Natural Theology

Collected Readings

Natural Theology

Collected Readings

Jean W. Rioux
Benedictine College

Wipf & Stock
PUBLISHERS
Eugene, Oregon

Wipf and Stock Publishers
199 W. 8th Avenue
Eugene, Oregon 97401
Www.wipfandstock.com

Natural Theology: Collected Readings
By Jean W. Rioux
Copyright © 2004 by Jean W. Rioux
ISBN: 1-59244-719-8

Contents

Chronology / vii
Outline / ix-x
Cross-Listing: *Summa Theologiae* to *Summa Contra Gentiles* / xi-xiii
Acknowledgments / xv

I. Ancient / 1

    1. Plato
       Meno, 96d-100b / 1
       Laws, Book X, 884-896 / 7

    2. Aristotle
       Posterior Analytics, II.1-2 / 15
       Posterior Analytics, I. 13 / 16
       Physics, VII. 1 / 16
       Physics, VIII. 5 / 19
       Metaphysics, II. 2 / 21
       Metaphysics, II. 1 / 21
       Metaphysics, IV. 4 / 22

II. Medieval /

    1. John Damascene
       On the Orthodox Faith, I. 3 / 23

    2. Anselm of Canterbury
       Proslogion, Chapter 2 / 23

    3. Gaunilon
       Pro Insipiente / 24

    4. Thomas Aquinas
       Commentary on the Metaphysics, Introduction / 27
       Commentary on the Posterior Analytics, II, 1 / 29
       Summa Theologiae, Ia, Questions 1 and 2 / 34

III. Modern and Contemporary /

1. René Descartes
    Meditations on First Philosophy: Meditation V / 47

2. Blaise Pascal
    Pensées, Section III: *Of the Necessity of the Wager* / 49

3. John Locke
    Essay Concerning Human Understanding, IV, 10 / 55

4. David Hume
    Dialogues Concerning Natural Religion, Part 8 / 59

5. Immanuel Kant
    Critique of Pure Reason: Transcendental Dialectic, II, 3, §§ 4-7 / 65

6. William Paley
    Natural Theology, chapters 1-2 / 81

7. Ludwig Feuerbach
    The Essence of Christianity, Chapter 1 / 91

8. Bertrand Russell
    "*Why I Am Not A Christian*" / 97

9. Michael J. Behe
    "*Molecular Machines: Experimental Support for the Design Inference*" / 105

Chronology

Plato	430-347 B.C.
Aristotle	384-322 B.C.
John Damascene (John of Damascus)	676-754?
Anselm of Canterbury	1033-1109
Gaunilon	(eleventh century)
Thomas Aquinas	1225-1275
René Descartes	1596-1650
Blaise Pascal	1623-1662
John Locke	1632-1704
David Hume	1711-1776
Immanuel Kant	1724-1804
William Paley	1743-1805
Ludwig Feuerbach	1804-1872
Bertrand Russell	1872-1970
Michael Behe	(contemporary)

Outline

I   Preliminaries to Doing Natural Theology Proper
  A   Introductory Material
    1   What is Natural Theology? How does it differ from Revealed Theology? To prove that God exists does not directly pertain to Natural Theology.
       Plato, *Meno*, 96d-100b
       Disputed Questions on Truth, 14, 1-2, 9
       Introduction to the Commentary on the Metaphysics
       Summa Theologiae, Ia, Question 1, articles 1 and 8
       Summa Contra Gentiles, I, 1-9
    2   Preliminaries to Proving that God Exists
      a   Advanced Logic
         Posterior Analytics, II. 1-2
         Commentary on the Posterior Analytics, II, 1
         Posterior Analytics, I. 13
      b   Ontological Arguments
         Anselm, *Proslogion*, Chapter 2 & Gaunilon, *Pro Insipiente*
         Descartes, *Meditations on First Philosophy*: Meditation V
         Summa Theologiae, Ia, Question 2, article 1
         Summa Contra Gentiles, I, 10-11
      c   Fideism: the Wager
         Pascal, *Pensées*, Section III: *Of the Necessity of the Wager*
         Summa Theologiae, Ia, Question 2, article 2
         Summa Contra Gentiles, I, 12
      d   Agnosticism and Atheism
         Kant, *Critique of Pure Reason:* Transcendental Dialectic, II, 3, §§ 4-7
         David Hume, *Dialogues Concerning Natural Religion*, Part 8
         Ludwig Feuerbach, *The Essence of Christianity*, Chapter 1
         Bertrand Russell, *"Why I Am Not A Christian"*

B Teleological and Cosmological Arguments
   Plato, *Laws*, Book X, 884-896
   Summa Contra Gentiles, I, 13
   (1) Aristotle, *Physics*, VII. 1
   (2) Aristotle, *Physics*, VIII. 5
   (3) Aristotle, *Metaphysics*, II. 2
   (4) Aristotle, *Metaphysics*, II. 1 and IV. 4
   (5) Damascene, *De Fide Orthodoxa*, I, 3
   Summa Theologiae, Ia, Question 2, article 3
   John Locke, *Essay Concerning Human Understanding*, IV, 10
   William Paley, *Natural Theology*, 1-2
   Michael Behe, *Molecular Machines: Experimental Support for the Design Inference*

II Understanding God's Nature and the Divine Attributes
   Summa Contra Gentiles, I, 14-102
   Summa Theologiae (selections)

Cross-Listing

SCG Chapter	Question and article from ST, Ia		
1			
2			
3	12, 4	14, 3	
4	1, 1		
5	1, 1		
6			
7			
8			
9	1, 8		
10	2, 1		
11	2, 1		
12	2, 2		
13	2, 3	9, 1	
14	9, 1		
15	2, 3	10, 2	
16	2, 3	3, 7	25, 1
17	3, 2	3, 8	
18	3, 7		
19			
20	3, 1		
21	3, 3		
22	3, 4		
23	3, 6		
24			
25	3, 5		
26	3, 8		
27	3, 8		
28	4, 1	4, 2	
29	4, 3		
30	13, 3		
31	4, 2	13, 2	
32	13, 5		
33	13, 5		
34	13, 5	13, 6	
35	13, 4		

36	13, 12			
37	6, 1			
38	6, 3			
39				
40	5, 4	6, 4		
41	6, 2			
42	11, 3			
43	7, 1	25, 2		
44	2, 3	14, 1		
45	14, 4			
46				
47	14, 2			
48	14, 5			
49	14, 5			
50	14, 6	14, 11		
51				
52	3, 4			
53				
54	15, 2			
55	14, 7	19, 2		
56	19, 2			
57	14, 7	19, 2		
58	14, 14			
59	14, 14	16, 2	16, 5	17, 3
60	16, 1			
61				
62				
63	14, 11			
64				
65	14, 11			
66	14, 9			
67	14, 13			
68				
69	14, 12			
70				
71	14, 10			
72	19, 1			
73	19, 1			

Cross-Listing

74				
75				
76	22, 3			
77	22, 3			
78				
79				
80	19, 3			
81	19, 3			
82	19, 3	19, 7		
83	19, 3	22, 3		
84	25, 3			
85	19, 8			
86	19, 5			
87	19, 5			
88	19, 10			
89				
90				
91	20, 1	20, 2	20, 3	21, 3
92				
93	21, 1			
94	22, 3			
95	19, 9			
96	19, 9			
97	18, 1	18, 3		
98	18, 2	18, 3		
99				
100	26, 1			
101				
102	26, 4			

Acknowledgments

Excerpt from Plato's *Laws, Meno*, translated by Benjamin Jowett, 1871.

Excerpts from Aristotle's *Posterior Analytics, Physics*, and *Metaphysics*, translated by Jean W. Rioux. © 1989 Jean W. Rioux.

Excerpt from John Damascene's *On the Orthodox Faith*, translated by Jean W. Rioux. © 1989 Jean W. Rioux.

Excerpt from Anselm of Canterbury's *Proslogion*, translated by Jean W. Rioux. © 1989 Jean W. Rioux.

Excerpt from Gaunilon's *Pro Insipiente*, translated by Jean W. Rioux. © 1989 Jean W. Rioux.

Excerpts from Thomas Aquinas' *Commentary on the Posterior Analytics of Aristotle*, and *Commentary on the Metaphysics of Aristotle*, translated by Jean W. Rioux. © 1989 Jean W. Rioux.

Excerpts from Thomas Aquinas' *Summa Theologica*, translated by Fathers of the English Dominican Province, 1947.

Excerpts from René Descartes' *Meditations on First Philosophy*, translated by John Veitch, 1901.

Excerpts from Blaise Pascal's *Pensées*, translated by W. F. Trotter, 1908.

Excerpts from Immanuel Kant's *Critique of Pure Reason*, translated by F. Max Müller, 1896.

Excerpt from Ludwig Feuerbach's *Essence of Christianity*, translated by George Eliot, 1854.

Plato, *Meno*, 96d-100b

I am afraid, Meno, that you and I are not good for much, and that Gorgias has been as poor an educator of you as Prodicus has been of me. Certainly we shall have to look to ourselves, and try to find some one who will help to improve us. This I say, because I observe that in the previous discussion none of us remarked that right and good action is possible to man under other guidance than that of knowledge;—and indeed if this be denied, there is no seeing how there can be any good men at all.

How do you mean, Socrates?

I mean this—that good men must necessarily be useful or profitable. Were we not right in admitting that?

Yes.

And in supposing that they will be useful only if they are true guides of action—in that we were also right?

Yes.

But we do not seem to have been right in saying that knowledge only was the right and good guide of action.

What do you mean by the word 'right'?

I will explain. If a man knew the way to Larisa, or anywhere else, and went to the place and led others thither, would he not be a right and good guide?

Certainly.

And a person who had a right opinion about the way, but had never been and did not know, might be a good guide also, might he not?

Certainly.

And while he has true opinion about that which the other knows, he will be just as good a guide if he thinks the truth, as if he knows the truth?

Exactly.

Then true opinion is as good a guide to correct action as wisdom; and that was the point which we omitted in our speculation about the nature of virtue, when we said that wisdom only is the guide of right action; whereas there is also right opinion.

True.

Then right opinion is not less useful than knowledge?

The difference, Socrates, is only that he who has knowledge will always be right; but he who has right opinion will sometimes be right, and sometimes not right.

What do you mean? Can he be wrong who has right opinion, as long as he has right opinion?

I admit the cogency of that, and therefore, Socrates, allowing this, I wonder that knowledge should be preferred to right opinion—or why they should ever differ.

And shall I explain this wonder to you?

Do tell me.

You would not wonder if you had ever observed the images of Daedalus; but perhaps you have not got them in your country?

Why do you refer to them?

Because they require to be fastened in order to keep them, and if they are not fastened they will run away.

Well, what of that?

I mean to say that it is not much use possessing one of them if they are at liberty, for they will walk off like runaway slaves; but when fastened, they are of great value, for they are really beautiful works of art. Now this is an illustration of the nature of true opinion: while they abide with us they are beautiful and fruitful, but they run away out of the human soul, and do not remain long, and therefore they are not of much value until they are fastened by the tie of the cause; and this fastening of them, friend Meno, is recollection, as has been already agreed by us. But when they are bound, in the first place, they are abiding. And this is why knowledge is more honorable and excellent than true opinion, because fastened by a chain.

Yes indeed, Socrates, that I should conjecture to be the truth.

I too speak not as one who knows; and yet that knowledge differs from true opinion is not a matter of conjecture with me. There are not many things which I should affirm that I knew, but that is most certainly one of them.

You are right, Socrates.

And am I not right also in saying that true opinion is as good a guide in the performance of an action as knowledge?

That also appears to me to be true.

Then right opinion is not a whit inferior to knowledge, or less useful in action; nor is the man who has right opinion inferior to him who has knowledge?

That is true.

And surely the good man has been acknowledged by us to be useful?

Yes.

Seeing then that men become good and useful to states, not only because they have knowledge, but because they have right opinion, and neither knowledge nor right opinion is given to man by nature or acquired by him—(do you think that either of them is given by nature?

Not I.)

Then if they are not given by nature, neither are the good by nature good?

Certainly not.

And nature being excluded, the next question was whether virtue is acquired by teaching?

Yes.

If virtue was wisdom, then, as we thought, it was taught?

Yes.

And if it was taught it was wisdom?

Certainly.

And if there were teachers, it might be taught; and if there were not teachers, not?

True.

But surely we acknowledged that there were no teachers of virtue?

Yes.

Then we acknowledged that it was not taught, and was not wisdom?

Certainly.

And yet we admitted that it was a good?

Yes.

And the right guide is useful and good?

Certainly.

And the only right guides are knowledge and true opinion—these are the guides of man; for things which happen by chance are not under the guidance of man: but the guides of man are true opinion and knowledge.

I think so too.

But if virtue is not taught, neither is virtue knowledge.

Clearly not.

And therefore not by any wisdom, and not because they were wise, did Themistocles and those others of whom Anytus spoke govern states. And this was the reason why they were unable to make others like themselves—because their virtue was not grounded on knowledge.

That is probably true, Socrates.

But if not by knowledge, the only alternative which remains is that statesmen must have guided states by right opinion, which is in politics what divination is in religion; for diviners and also prophets say many things truly, but they know not what they say.

Very true.

And may we not, Meno, truly call those men divine who, having no understanding, yet succeed in many a grand deed and word?

Certainly.

Then we shall also be right in calling those divine whom we were just now speaking of as diviners and prophets, as well as all poets. Yes, and statesmen above all may be said to be divine and illumined, being inspired and possessed of God, in which condition they say many grand things, not knowing what they say.

Yes.

And the women too, Meno, call good men divine; and the Spartans, when they praise a good man, say 'that he is a divine man'.

And I think, Socrates, that they are right; although very likely our friend Anytus may take offense at the name.

I do not care; as for Anytus, there will be another opportunity of talking with him. To sum up our inquiry—the result seems to be, if we are at all right in our view, that virtue is neither natural nor acquired, but an instinct given by God to the virtuous. Nor is the instinct accompanied by reason, unless there may be supposed to be among statesmen any one who is also the educator of statesmen. And if there by such an one, he may be said to be among the living what Tiresias was among the dead, who 'alone', according to Homer, 'of those in the world below, has understanding; but the rest flit as shadows'.

That is excellent, Socrates.

Then, Meno, the conclusion is that virtue comes to the virtuous by the gift of God. But we shall never know the certain truth until, before asking how virtue is given, we inquire into the actual nature of virtue. I fear that I must go away, but do you, now that you are persuaded yourself, persuade our friend Anytus. And don't let him be so exasperated; for if you can persuade him you will have done some service to the Athenian people.

Plato, *Laws*, Book X, 884-896

Athenian. And now having spoken of assaults, let us sum up all acts of violence under a single law, which shall be as follows:—No one shall take or carry away any of his neighbor's goods, neither shall he use anything which is his neighbor's without the consent of the owner; for these are the offenses which are and have been, and will ever be, the source of all the aforesaid evils. The greatest of them are excesses and insolences of youth, and are offenses against the greatest when they are done against religion; and especially great when in violation of public and holy rites, or of the partly-common rites in which tribes and phratries share; and in the second degree great when they are committed against private rites and sepulchers, and in the third degree (not to repeat the acts formerly mentioned), when insults are offered to parents; the fourth kind of violence is when any one, regardless of the authority of the rulers, takes or carries away or makes use of anything which belongs to them, not having their consent; and the fifth kind is when the violation of the civil rights of an individual demands reparation. There should be a common law embracing all these cases. For we have already said in general terms what shall be the punishment of the sacrilege, whether fraudulent or violent, and now we have to determine what is to be the punishment of those who speak or act insolently toward the Gods. But first we must give them an admonition which may be in the following terms:—No one who in obedience to the laws believed that there were Gods, ever intentionally do any unholy act, or uttered any unlawful word; but he who did must have supposed one of three things,—either that they did not exist,—which is the first possibility, or secondly, that, if they did, they took no care of man, or thirdly, that they were easily appeased and turned aside from their purpose by sacrifices and prayers.

Cleinias. What shall we say or do to these persons?

Athenian. My good friend, let us first hear the jests which I suspect that they in their superiority will utter against us.

Cleinias. What jests?

Athenian. They will make some irreverent speech of this sort:—'O inhabitants of Athens, and Sparta, and Cnosus,' they will reply, 'in that you speak truly; for some of us deny the very existence of the Gods, while others, as you say, are of opinion that they do not care about us; and others that they are turned from their course by gifts. Now we have a right to claim, as you yourself allowed, in the matter of laws, that before you are hard upon us and threaten us, you should argue with us and convince us—you should first attempt to teach and persuade us that there are Gods by reasonable evidences, and also that they are too good to be unrighteous, or to be propitiated, or turned from their course by gifts. For when we hear such things said of them by those who are esteemed to be the best of poets, and orators, and prophets, and priests, and by innumerable others, the thoughts of most of us are not set upon abstaining from unrighteous acts, but upon doing them and atoning for them. When lawgivers profess that they are gentle and not stern, we think that they should first of all use persuasion to us, and show us the existence of Gods, if not in a better manner than other men, at any rate in a truer; and who knows but that we shall hearken to you? If then our request is a fair one, please to accept our challenge.'

Cleinias. But is there any difficulty in proving the existence of the Gods?

Athenian. How would you prove it?

Cleinias. How? In the first place, the earth and the sun, and the stars and the universe, and the fair order of the seasons, and the division of them into years and months, furnish proofs of their existence; and also there is the fact that all Hellenes and barbarians believe in them.

Athenian. I fear, my sweet friend, though I will not say that I much regard, the contempt with which the profane will be likely to assail us. For you do not understand the nature of their complaint, and you fancy that they rush into impiety only from a love of sensual pleasure.

Cleinias. Why, Stranger, what other reason is there?

Athenian. One which you who live in a different atmosphere would never guess.

Cleinias. What is it?

Athenian. A very grievous sort of ignorance which is imagined to be the greatest wisdom.

Cleinias. What do you mean?

Athenian. At Athens there are tales preserved in writing which the virtue of your state, as I am informed, refuses to admit. They speak of the Gods in prose as well as verse, and the oldest of them tell of the origins of the heavens and of the world, and not far from the beginning of their story they proceed to narrate the birth of the Gods, and how after they were born they behaved to one another. Whether these stories have in other ways a good or a bad influence, I should not like to be severe upon them, because they are ancient; but, looking at them with reference to the duties of children to their parents, I cannot praise them, or think that they are useful, or at all true. Of the words of the ancients I have nothing more to say; and I should wish to say of them only what is pleasing to the Gods. But as to our younger generation and their wisdom, I cannot let them off when they do mischief. For do but mark the effect of their words: when you and I argue for the existence of the Gods, and produce the sun, moon, stars, and earth, claiming for them a divine being, if we would listen to the aforesaid philosophers we should say that they are earth and stones only, which can have no care at all of human affairs, and that all religion is a cooking up of words and a make-believe...

Cleinias. What a dreadful picture, Stranger, have you given, and how great is the injury which is thus inflicted on young men to the ruin both of states and families!

Athenian. True, Cleinias; but then what should the lawgiver do when this evil is of long standing? should he only rise up in the state and threaten all mankind, proclaiming that if they will not say and think that the Gods are such as the law ordains (and this may be extended generally to the honorable, the just, and to all the highest things, and to all that relates to virtue and vice), and if they will not make their actions conform to the copy which the law gives them, then he who refuses to obey the law shall die, or suffer stripes and bonds, or privation of citizenship, or in some cases be punished by loss of property and exile? Should he not rather, when he is making laws for men, at the same time infuse the spirit of persuasion into his words, and mitigate the severity of them as far as he can?

Cleinias. Why, Stranger, if such persuasion be at all possible, then a legislator who has anything in him ought never to weary of persuading men; he ought to leave nothing unsaid in support of the ancient opinion that there are Gods, and of all those other truths which you were just now mentioning; he ought to support the law and also art, and acknowledge that both alike exist by nature, and no less than nature, if they are the creations of mind in accordance with right reason, as you appear to me to maintain, and I am disposed to agree with you in thinking.

Athenian. Yes, my enthusiastic Cleinias; but are not these things when spoken to a multitude hard to be understood, not to mention that they take up a dismal length of time?

Cleinias. Why, Stranger, shall we, whose patience failed not when drinking or music were the themes of discourse, weary now of discoursing about the Gods, and about Divine things? And the greatest help to rational legislation is that the laws when once written down are always at rest; they can be put to the test at any future time, and therefore, if on first hearing they seem difficult, there is no reason for apprehension about them, because any man however dull can go over them and consider them again and again; nor if they are tedious but useful, is there any reason or religion, as it seems to me, in any man refusing to maintain the principles of them to the utmost of his power.

Megillus. Stranger, I like what Cleinias is saying.

Athenian. Yes, Megillus, and we should do as he proposes; for if impious discourses were not scattered, as I may say, throughout the world, there would have been no need for any vindication of the existence of the Gods—but seeing that they are spread far and wide, such arguments are needed; and who should come to the rescue of the greatest laws, when they are being undermined by bad men, but the legislator himself?

Megillus. There is no more proper champion of them.

Athenian. Well, then, tell me, Cleinias,—for I must ask you to be my partner,—does not he who talks in this way conceive fire and water and earth and air to be the first elements of all things? these he calls nature, and out of these he supposes the soul to be formed afterwards; and this is not a mere conjecture of ours about his meaning, but is what he really means.

Cleinias. Very true.

Athenian. Then, by Heaven, we have discovered the source of this vain opinion of all those physical investigators; and I would have you examine their arguments with the utmost care, for their impiety is a very serious matter; they not only make a bad and mistaken use of argument, but they lead away the minds of others: that is my opinion of them.

Cleinias. You are right, but I should like to know how this happens.

Athenian. I fear that the argument may seem singular.

Cleinias. Do not hesitate, Stranger; I see that you are afraid of such a discussion carrying you beyond the limits of legislation. But if there be no other way of showing our agreement in the belief that there are Gods, of whom the law is said now to approve, let us take this way, my good sir.

Athenian. Then I suppose that I must repeat the singular argument of those who manufacture the soul according to their own impious notions; they affirm that which is the first cause of the generation and destruction of all things, to be not first, but last, and that which is last to be first, and hence they have fallen into error about the true nature of the Gods.

Cleinias. Still I do not understand you.

Athenian. Nearly all of them, my friends, seem to be ignorant of the nature and power of the soul, especially in what relates to her origin: they do not know that she is among the first of things, and before all bodies, and is the chief author of their changes and transpositions. And if this is true, and if the soul is older than the body, must not the things which are of the soul's kindred be of necessity prior to those which appertain to the body?

Cleinias. Certainly.

Athenian. Then thought and attention and mind and art and law will be prior to that which is hard and soft and heavy and light; and the great and primitive works and actions will be works of art; they will be the first, and after them will come nature and works of nature, which however is a wrong term for men to apply to them; these will follow, and will be under the government of art and mind.

Cleinias. But why is the word 'nature' wrong?

Athenian. Because those who use the term mean to say that nature is the first creative power; but if the soul turned out to be the first primeval element, and not fire or air, then in the truest sense and beyond other things the soul may be said to exist by nature; and this would be true if you proved that the soul is older than the body, but not otherwise.

Cleinias. You are quite right.

Athenian. Shall we, then, take this as the next point to which our attention should be directed?

Cleinias. By all means.

Athenian. Come, then, and if ever we are to call upon the Gods, let us call upon them now in all seriousness to come to the demonstration of their own existence. And so holding fast to the rope we will venture upon the depths of the argument. When questions of this sort are asked of me, my safest answer would appear to be as follows:—Some one says to me, 'O Stranger, are all things at rest and nothing in motion, or is the exact opposite of this true, or are some things in motion and others at rest?'—To this I shall reply that some things are in motion and others at rest. 'And do not things which move move in a place, and are not the things which are at rest at rest in a place?' Certainly. 'And some move or rest in one place and some in more places than one?' You mean to say, we shall rejoin, that those things which rest at the center move in one place, just as the circumference goes round of globes which are said to be at rest? 'Yes.' And we observe that, in the revolution, the motion which carries round the larger and the lesser circle at the same time is proportionally distributed to greater and smaller, and is greater and smaller in a certain proportion. Here is a wonder which might be thought an impossibility, that the same motion should impart swiftness and slowness in due proportion to larger and lesser circles. 'Very true.' And when you speak of bodies moving in many places, you seem to me to mean those which move from one place to another, and sometimes have one center of motion and sometimes more than one because they turn upon their axis; and whenever they meet anything, if it be stationary, they are divided by it; but if they get in the midst between bodies which are approaching and moving towards the same spot from opposite directions, they unite with them. 'I admit the truth of what you are saying.' Also when they unite they grow, and when they are divided they waste away,—that is, supposing the constitution of each to remain, or if that fails, then there is a second reason of their dissolution. 'And when are all things created and how?' Clearly, they are created when the first principle receives increase and attains to the second dimension, and from this arrives at the one which is neighbor to this, and after reaching the third principle becomes perceptible to sense. Everything which is thus changing and moving is in process of generation; only when at rest has it real existence, but when passing into another state it is destroyed utterly. Have we not mentioned all motions that there are, and comprehended them under their kinds and numbered them with the exception, my friends, of two?

Cleinias. Which are they?

Athenian. Just the two, with which our present inquiry is concerned.

Cleinias. Speak plainer.

Athenian. I suppose that our inquiry has reference to the soul?

Cleinias. Very true.

Athenian. Let us assume that there is a motion able to move other things, but not to move itself;—that is one kind; and there is another kind which can move itself as well as other things, working in composition and decomposition, by increase and diminution and generation and destruction,—that is also one of the many kinds of motion.

Cleinias. Granted.

Athenian. And we will assume that which is moved by other, and is changed by other, to be the ninth, and that which changes itself and others, and is coincident with every action and every passion, and is the true principle of change and motion in all that is,—that we shall be inclined to call the tenth.

Cleinias. Certainly.

Athenian. And which of these ten motions ought we to prefer as being the mightiest and most efficient?

Cleinias. I must say that the motion which is able to move itself is ten thousand times superior to all the others.

Athenian. Very good; but may I make one or two corrections in what I have been saying?

Cleinias. What are they?

Athenian. When I spoke of the tenth sort of motion, that was not quite correct.

Cleinias. What was the error?

Athenian. According to the true order, the tenth was really the first in generation and power; then follows the second, which was strangely enough termed the ninth by us.

Cleinias. What do you mean?

Athenian. I mean this: when one thing changes another, and that another, of such will there be any primary changing element? How can a thing which is moved by another ever be the beginning of change? Impossible. But when the self-moved changes another, and that again another, and thus thousands upon tens of thousands of bodies are set in motion, must not the principle of all this motion be the change of the self-moving principle?

Cleinias. Very true, and I quite agree.

Athenian. Or, to put the question in another way, making answer to ourselves:—If, as most of these philosophers have the audacity to affirm, all things were at rest in one mass, which of the above-mentioned principles of motion would first spring up among them?

Cleinias. Clearly, the self-moving; for there could be no change in them arising out of any external cause; the change must first take place in themselves.

Athenian. Then we must say that self-motion being the origin of all motions, and the first which arises among things at rest as well as among things in motion, is the eldest and mightiness principle of change, and that which is changed by another and yet moves another is second.

Aristotle, *Posterior Analytics*, II.1-2

1   The questions we ask are equal in number to the things we can know. Now we ask four things: whether it is so, why it is, whether it is, what it is. For when we ask whether it is thus or otherwise, placing into number, as whether the sun is eclipsed or not, we ask whether it is so [*quia*]. A sign of this: when we see that it [the sun] is eclipsed, we cease [our inquiry:] and if we know from the start that it is eclipsed, we do not as whether [it is]. But when we know whether it is so [*quia*,] we then ask why, as those who know that [the sun] is eclipsed and that the earth is moved ask why it is eclipsed or why it is moved. So much for these [questions.] We also ask in another way, for example, whether a centaur or God is or not: and I say whether it is or not simply, not whether it is or is not white. And when we know that it is, we then ask what it is, as: what is God, or, what is man?

2   Such, then, and so many, are the things which we seek and which we, when we have discovered them, know. Now when we ask whether it is so [*quia*] or whether it is simply we are asking whether this has a middle [term] or not: but when, already knowing whether it is so or whether it is simply, either in part or simply, we then ask why or what it is, and then we are asking what the middle is. ... In all these questions one must ask either whether there is a middle or what the middle is. For the middle is a cause, and this is sought in all things. Is [the sun] eclipsed? Is there some cause or not? And beyond these things, when we know whether something is, we then ask what it is. For the cause of being (not being such or otherwise but being taken simply, substance) and the cause of being (not being taken simply but being some one of those things which are either *per se* or *per accidens*) is the middle. Now, on the one hand, I call that which is, simply speaking, the subject, as the moon or the earth or the sun or the triangle, while, on the other hand, [there is] what that thing is, as eclipse, equality, inequality, interposed or not interposed...

That our question is about the middle [term] is clear whenever the middle is sensible. For, when we do not know, we ask, as of the eclipse, is it or not? Yet if we were upon the moon, we would have asked neither whether it happened nor why, but [these] would be immediately clear. For the universal becomes known to us through sensation. For sensation [tells us] that [the earth] is now interposed (for it is clear that [the moon] is now eclipsed:) and thus does the universal come about.

Aristotle, Posterior Analytics, I. 13

To understand that it is and to understand why it is differ... in another way through the middle, not through the cause but through the more-known of opposites. For nothing prevents the more-known of two opposites to be that one which is not the cause, such that the demonstration will be through this, as that the planets are near because they do not twinkle. Let C be the planets, B be not twinkling, and A be nearness. It is true to say B of C: for the planets do not twinkle. And [it is true] also [to say] A of B: for what does not twinkle is near (and let this have been shown through induction or sensation.) Now it is necessary that A inhere in C, so that it has been demonstrated that the planets are near. Now this syllogism is not of the why but of the that. For it is not because [the planets] do not twinkle that they are near, but they do not twinkle because they are near.

Aristotle, Physics, VII. 1

Everything which is moved must be moved by something: for if it does not have its own principle of motion, it is clear that it is moved by another (for the mover will be another thing.) But if [the principle of its motion] is in itself, let AB be that which is moved *per se*, and not because some part of it is moved. First, then, the assumption that AB is moved by itself because the whole is moved by nothing outside of it is just as if, with KL moving LM and itself being moved, someone were to say that KM is not moved by something because it is not clear whether it is a mover or whether it is moved: further, it is not necessary that what is being moved (but not by something) stops because some other thing has come to rest, but if something which is moved rests because some other thing has stopped, it is necessary that the former is moved by something. Given this, everything which is moved must be moved by something. For since we assumed that AB is moved, it is necessary that it is divisible: for everything which is moved is divisible. Let [AB] be divided at C. Now if CB is not moved then AB will not be moved: for if it were moved, it is clear that AC would move while CB was at rest, so that [AB] would not be moved *per se* and first. Therefore it is necessary that while CB is not moved AB is at rest. But it was agreed that whatever is at rest while some [other] thing is not moved is moved by something, so that everything which is moved is necessarily moved by something: for that which is moved will be continuously divisible, and while a part is not being moved it is necessary that the whole is at rest.

Since, then, everything which is moved must be moved by something, if something is moved according to motion in place by another which is moved, and again the mover is moved by another which is moved, and that one by another, always in this way, it is necessary that there be a first mover, and that it not proceed into the infinite: for let it be not so, but let it be made infinite. And let A be moved by B, and B by C, and C by D, and always what is next by what is beyond that. Now since it is given that the mover moves what is moved, and the motion of what is moved and that of the mover must occur at the same time (for the mover moves [what is moved] and what is moved is moved at the same time:) then it is clear that the motion of A and of B and of C and of each of the movers and things which are moved will be simultaneous. Let there be the motion of each, and let that of A be E, that of B be F, and those of C and D be G and H. For even though each is always moved by each, we may take the motion of each in this way as one in number: for every motion is from something to something, and it is not infinite with respect to its extremes. Now I call 'one in number' a motion which proceeds from something one and the same in number to something one in number in a time one and the same in number. For motion may be the same in kind and in species and in number: in kind, on the one hand, that which is of the same category, as of substance or of quality, in species, that which is from something the same in species to something the same in species, as from white to black or from a good to an evil not differing in species, and in number, that which is from what is one in number to what is one in number in the same time, as from this white to this black, or from this place to that place, in this time: for if it is in another [time,] the motion will not be one in number but in species. We have spoken of these things already.

Let us assume the time in which A moved according to its motion, and let it be K. Now when the motion of A is completed the time will also be completed. And since the movers and the things which are moved are infinite, the motion EFGH, that of the whole, will also be infinite: for it may be assumed that A and B and the others are equal to each other, or it may be assumed that they are greater than the others, so that if they are either equal to or greater than the others, in either case the whole is infinite: for we assume what is possible. But since A and each of the others moves [another] at the same time, the whole motion will be in the same time as that of A: but that of A was in a completed [time:] so that the infinite [will move] in a finite [time;] but this is impossible. ...for it was assumed that an infinite motion [occurred] in a finite time, not of one thing, but of many. Whence it happens also with these things: for each is moved according to its motion, but that any things are moved at the same time is not impossible. But if that which is first moving is [moving] according to place, and it is a bodily motion, it is necessary that it is either touching or continuous with what is being moved, just as we see with all [the movers and things which are moved,] it is necessary that the things which are moved and the movers be either touching or continuous with one another, so that there is a certain one [made up] of all of them. Now this [one] is either finite or infinite; it makes no difference for the moment: for the motion will be wholly infinite, being of things which are in finite, for it was assumed that they are either equal to or greater than each other: for what is possible we may take as being so.

Now whether ABCD is something finite or infinite, the motion EFGH moves in time K, which in finite, and infinite happens to be traversed in a finite time, whether this [traversing] is finite or infinite. And each is impossible: so that it is necessary to make a stand and [say] that there is something which is a first mover and something which is first being moved: for it makes no difference that the impossible comes about from a hypothesis: for the hypothesis assumed was possible, and nothing impossible should come about from a possible assumption.

Aristotle, *Physics*, VIII. 5

It is necessary that everything which is moved is divisible into [parts] which are always divisible: for this has already been shown in the general writings concerning nature, that everything which is essentially moved is continuous. But it is impossible that that which moves itself moves itself wholly: for the whole would have and would bring about the same motion according to place, being one and indivisible in species, and it would both be altered and alter, so that one would both teach and be taught at the same time, and one would be both healing and being healed with respect to the same health. Further, it was stated that the movable is moved: but this is moved potentially, not actually. But it is the potential which proceeds to actuality, and motion is the incomplete actuality of the movable. Yet the mover is already actual, for example, what is hot heats, and what generates [another] has the form wholly. So that the same thing with respect to the same thing will be both hot and not hot at the same time. And likewise with each of the others, in which the mover and what is moved necessarily have the same name. Therefore, of that which moves itself, one [part] moves and the other [part] is moved.

All things that are moved are moved by something. And this may be in two ways: for the mover may not [move] through itself, but the mover [may move] through another which moves, (or [it may move] through itself,) and (it may do this) either as immediately next to the effect or through many things, as the stick moves the stone and it is moved by the hand which is moved by the man, though he is not moved by another; now both the last and the first of the movers are said by us to move [something,] but more the first: for it moves the last, but the last does not [move] the first, and without the first the last will not move [something,] but [the first] can move without the last, as the stick will not move [the stone] without being moved by the man.

Now if it is necessary that everything which is moved is moved by something, and it is either moved by another which is itself moved or it is not, and if it is moved by another it is necessary that there be some first mover which is not [moved] by another, but if [it is not moved by another] it is first, another is not necessary. (For it is impossible that movers and things which are moved by another proceed into the infinite: for in an infinite there is no first.) Now if all things which are moved are moved by something, but the first mover is moved, but not by another, it is necessary that it move itself.

Every mover both moves something and moves by means of something. For either the mover moves by means of itself or by means of another, as a man [might move something] by means of himself or by means of a stick, and the wind knocked [something] down either by itself or by means of the stone which it loosened. But it is impossible for that by means of which something moves [something] to move [something] without being moved by that which moves itself: but if it moves itself by means of itself, it is not necessary that there be another by means of which it moves [another,] but if that by means of which it moves [something] is another, there is something which it moves, not by means of something [other than itself,] else there will be a [series] into the infinite. Now if it moves something which is moved, there must be a stop, and it cannot proceed to the infinite: for if the stick moves something because it is moved by the hand, the hand moves the stick: but if some other thing moves [something] by means of the hand, there is something which is a mover of it other than itself. When that by which something moves [something] is always other [than the mover,] there must be some prior mover [which moves] by means of itself. Now if [the prior mover] is moved, but there is not another [mover] moving it, it must move itself. So that, by this argument, either what is moved is moved by something which moves itself or one arrives [eventually] at such a thing. ...

If everything which is moved is moved by something which is moved, either this happens by accident, so that what is moved moves [another] yet not insofar as it itself is moved, or not, but essentially. First then, if it is by accident, it is not necessary that the mover is moved. And if this is so, it is possible that, at some time, no beings would be moved: for the accidental is not necessary, but is able not to be. If we suppose what is able to be, nothing impossible should happen (though perhaps something false would.) But that there be no motion is impossible: for it was shown earlier that it is necessary that motion always be.

And this also comes about reasonably. For there must be three things: what is moved, the mover, and that by means of which [the mover] moves [another.] Now that which is moved must be moved, but it is not necessary that it move [another:] but that by means of which [the mover] moves both moves and is moved (for it changes [what is moved] at the same time and according to the same being in motion: and this is clear among things which are moved according to place: for they must touch one another to some degree:) but that mover [which moves] in this way, such that it is not that by means of which [something] moves [another] is unmoved. For since we see the effect, that which can be moved but which has no principle of motion, and that which is moved, but by another and not by itself, it is reasonable, as we call what is not necessary, that there be a third, which moves without being moved.

Aristotle, *Metaphysics*, II. 2

Of the intermediates, which are between what is last and what is prior, it is necessary that what is prior be a cause of what comes after it. For if we were to say which, of the three, is a cause, we would say the first: for it cannot be the last, since what comes at the end is [the cause of] nothing: nor is it the intermediate, for it [is the cause of] one. And it makes no difference whether the intermediate is one or many, infinite or finite. Now of this sort of infinite (and of the infinite generally) all the parts are intermediates in the same way, right down to the present. So that if there is no first, there is no cause whatsoever.

Aristotle, *Metaphysics*, II. 1

We cannot know truth without [knowing] the cause. Now that thing is itself the greatest according to which something common inheres in other things (as fire is the hottest, for it is the cause of heat in the others:) so that which is the cause of consequent things' being true is most true. Whence it is necessary that the principles of beings are always the truest: for they are not true [only] sometimes, nor is something [else] a cause of their being, rather they [are the cause of being] in others, so that just as each thing has being, so also [does it have] truth.

Aristotle, *Metaphysics*, IV. 4

However much all things are 'so' or 'not so', yet the greater and the less are in the nature of things: for we should not say that two and three are similarly even, nor are the one thinking that four is five and that four is one thousand equally wrong; but if [they are] not equally [wrong,] it is clear that one is less incorrect and do more true. Now, if what has more [of something] is nearer, then there should be something true which what is more true is nearer. And if there is not, there is still something more certain and truer.

Damascene, On the Orthodox Faith, I. 3

How could the contrary natures, such as fire, water, air, and earth, be combined into a single order, be mixed with each other and remain undiluted, were not some wholly actual power forcing them together and keeping them ever undiluted?

Anselm, *Proslogion*, Chapter 2

Therefore, Lord, you who give understanding to faith, give to me as much as you think is useful, that I may understand that you are as we believe and what we believe [you to be]. And we believe, in fact, that you are something than which nothing greater can be thought. Or, rather, is there no such nature, because "the fool said in his heart: there is no God" (Psalms xiv 1)? But certainly this very fool, when he hears what I say: 'something than which nothing greater can be thought', understands what he hears; and what he understands is in his intellect, even if he does not know that it exists. For it is one thing for something to be in the intellect, another that something is understood to be [exist]. For when a painter first considers what is going to be made, he has this thing in his intellect, yet he does not know that the thing, which he has not yet made, exists. But when he has painted it, he both has it in his intellect and understands that what he has made exists. And so even the fool has become convinced that something than which nothing greater can be thought is in the intellect, because he understands this when he hears it, and whatever is understood is in the intellect. And certainly that than which a greater cannot be thought cannot be in the intellect alone. For if it is in the intellect alone, it can be thought also [to be] in reality, which is greater. If, then, that than which a greater cannot be thought is in the intellect alone, that than which a greater cannot be thought is that than which a greater can be thought. But clearly this cannot be. Therefore there is no doubt that something than which a greater cannot be thought exists, both in the intellect and in reality.

Gaunilon, Pro Insipiente

When it is said in response to the one doubting whether there is, or to the one denying that there is, such a thing than which nothing greater can be thought:

Its existence is proved first because the one denying or doubting it already has it in his intellect when he hears that [a thing than which nothing greater can be thought] being said, and understands what is being said; and then, because what he understands cannot be in the intellect alone but must also be in reality, which is proved in this way: it is greater to exist in reality than to exist in the intellect alone, and if that were in the intellect alone, anything which is also in reality will be greater than that, and so what is greater than all will be less than some thing and it will not be greater than all, which is inconsistent at least; and so it is necessary that what is greater than all (which has already been shown to exist in the intellect) cannot be in the intellect alone, but must also exist in reality, since it would not otherwise be able to be greater than all.

Perhaps he [the fool] can respond:

To say that what is spoken is already in my intellect is no different from saying that I understand what is said: are there not many false things which I may be said to have in my intellect in a similar fashion which in no way exist in themselves, since I would understand, upon someone saying it, whatever he said? Unless, perhaps, such a thing was agreed to be such that it is able to be held in the understanding, but not as every false or doubtful thing is, and therefore I am not said to 'think' [cogitare] what is heard nor to have it 'in mind' [in cogitatione], but to understand [intelligere] and to have it in the understanding [in intellectu], because I would not be able to understand this unless by understanding it (that is, by comprehending, with scientific knowledge, that this very thing exists.)

Yet if this is so, first, to have to have something in mind, preceding it in time, will not be one thing, and to know that it exists, following it in time, will not be another; as does happen with the picture, which is first in the mind of the artist, then in the product.

Also, when that was said and heard, it is hardly believable that it cannot in some way be thought not to exist, as even God is able to be [thought not to exist]. For if one cannot [even think that God does not exist], then why was this entire disputation taken up against one who denies or doubts that there is such a nature?

Finally, that this thing is of such a sort that it cannot be perceived by an intellect without the thought of its undoubtable existence, this must be proved by some indubitable argument, and not by this one: that I already understand what is in my intellect when it is heard, in which I still think that there can be many other uncertain or even false things from someone whose spoken words I may have understood; and even more if I were to believe, (deceived, as often happens,) that which I do not yet believe.

Thomas Aquinas, *Commentary on the Metaphysics*, Introduction

Just as the Philosopher teaches in his Politics, when many things are ordered to one, it is necessary that one [among them] regulate or rule and that the others be regulated or be ruled. This is clear in the union of the soul and the body. For the soul naturally commands, while the body obeys. Similarly also among the powers of the soul: for the irascible and concupiscible powers are, in the natural order, regulated by the reason. Now all the sciences and arts are ordered to one thing, the perfection of man, which is his happiness. Whence it is necessary that one of those [arts and sciences] be the regulator of all the others, and this one will rightly claim the name of wisdom. For it is characteristic of one who is wise to bring order among others.

Now we are able to consider what this science is and with what sorts of things it is concerned if we diligently inquire into how someone is fit to rule. For, as the Philosopher said in the aforementioned work, men with vigorous minds are naturally the directors and rulers of others: while men who are strong in body but are lacking intellectually are naturally ruled; thus that science ought naturally to be the regulator of the others which is most intellectual. And this is the one which is concerned with those things which are most intelligible.

We are able to say something is 'most intelligible' in three ways:

First, from the order of understanding. For those things from which the intellect acquires certitude seem to be more intelligible. Whence, since the certitude of science is acquired by the intellect through the causes, [therefore] knowledge of the causes seems to be the most intellectual. Whence also that science which considers the first causes best seems to be the regulator of the others.

Secondly, from the comparison of the intellect to the senses. For since sensation is the understanding of particulars, the intellect seems to differ from it in this, that it comprehends universals. Whence that science is the most intellectual which is concerned with the most universal principles. These [principles] are being and those things which follow upon being, such as one and many, and potency and act. Yet [principles] of this sort ought not to remain altogether indeterminate, although without them a complete understanding of those things which are proper to some genus or species is not able to be gained. Nor ought they to be treated in some one of the particular sciences, since because every genus of being needs them in order that it may be understood, by like reasoning it must be treated in every single science. Whence it remains that [principles] of this sort ought to be treated in a single common science; which, since it is the most intellectual, is the regulator of the others.

Thirdly, from the very understanding of the intellect. For, since something has an intellective power from the fact that it is free from matter, it follows that those things are most intelligible which are the most separate from matter. For that which is understood [the intelligible] and the intellect must be proportionate and of one genus, since the intellect and what is actually intelligible are one. But those things are most separate from matter which are not only abstracted from 'signate' matter, 'as natural forms taken universally, about which natural science treats,' but also from sensible matter entirely. And [this] not only according to reason, as the mathematicals, but also according to their being, as God and the Intelligences. Whence that science which considers such things seems to be the most intellectual, and the prince or leader of the others.

This threefold consideration ought to be attributed, not to different, but to a single, science. For the aforementioned separated substances are universal and first causes of being. Now it belongs to the same science to consider the proper causes of some genus and the genus itself: just as the philosopher of nature considers the principles of natural body. Whence it is necessary that it pertain to the same science to consider the separated substances and common being, which is the genus of which the aforementioned substances are the common and universal causes.

Whence it appears that, although this science considers three things, it nevertheless does not consider each of them as a subject, but only common being. For that is the subject of a science whose causes and passions we are seeking, and not the causes themselves of the genus in question. For the understanding of the causes of some genus is the end to which the consideration in a science attains. Now although the subject of this science is common being, nevertheless it is said to be about all those things which are separate from matter according to their being and [according to] reason. Since not only are those which are never able to be in matter, such as God and the intellectual substances, said to be separate according to their being and [according to] reason, but also those things which are able to be without matter, such as common being.

Therefore we arrive at three names [for this science] according to the aforementioned three [properties,] from which the perfection of this science is reckoned. For it is called divine science or [natural] theology insofar as it considers the aforementioned substances. [It is called] Metaphysics, insofar as it considers being and those things which follow upon it. For those things which 'come after the physics' [*transphysica*] are discovered in the way of resolution, as the more common after the less common. And it is called First Philosophy, insofar as it considers the first causes of things. Thus it is clear what the subject of this science is, how it is related to the other sciences, and how it is named.

Thomas Aquinas, *Commentary on the Posterior Analytics*, II, 1

[Aristotle] first says that the number of questions [we ask] and of things which are known is equal. The reason for this is that scientific knowledge is understanding acquired through demonstration. It is necessary, however, to acquire knowledge of those things which were unknown through demonstration: and we ask questions about those things which we do not know. Whence it follows that those things which are asked are equal in number to those things which are known.

Now there are four things which are asked, namely, whether it is so [*quia*], why, whether it is, or what it is, to which four can be reduced whatever is questionable or knowable. ...

Then, when he says "For when we ask..." he makes the proposed questions manifest, and first the composite ones. In evidence of which it must be considered that, since scientific knowledge is only of that which is true, but truth is signified only through an enunciation, it is necessary that only the enunciation be [scientifically] knowable, and consequently questionable. Yet, as it is said in the second book of *On Interpretation*, the enunciation is formed in two ways. In one way, from the name and the verb without something joined [to it,] as when one says 'man is;' in another way, when some third thing is joined [to it,] as when one says 'man is white.'

A question which has been formulated, then, can be referred either to the first mode of enunciation, and thus it will be a simple question, as it were; or to the second mode, and thus it will be a composite question, so to speak, or one 'placing into number,' since it asks about the composition of two things.

Within this [latter] mode of enunciation, then, a question can be formulated in two ways. In one way, whether what is said is true. And he explains this question first, saying that when we ask about something whether it is this or that, (and thus we 'place into number,' in a certain way, in taking two things of which one is the predicate and the other the subject ; as, for example, when we ask whether the sun is eclipsed or not, or whether man is an animal or not,) we are then said to ask whether it is so [*quia*]: not in this way, insofar as what I call *quia* may be a mark or a sign of interrogation, but because we ask about this that we might know whether it is so. A sign of which is that, when we have found [the answer] through demonstration, we have ceased to ask; and if we knew this from the beginning, we do not ask whether it is so [at all.] For an inquiry does not end until that which is sought is had. And therefore since the question in which we ask whether this is that ends once one knows that this is so, it is manifest what a question of this sort is asking.

Then, when he says "For when we..." he makes the next question manifest, which question also 'places into number;' and he says that when we know whether this is so, we then ask why it is so. For example, when we know that the sun is eclipsed, or that the earth is moved in an earthquake, we then ask why the sun is eclipsed or why the earth moves. Therefore we ask this is this way: 'placing into number.'

Then, when he says "We also ask..." he manifests the other two questions, which do not 'place into number,' but are simple. And he says that we ask about certain things in a way other than those already mentioned: namely, when we do not 'place into number:' as if we would ask whether a centaur is or is not: for here one asks about the centaur whether it is simply, one does not ask whether the centaur is such (for example, white,) or not. And just as when we know whether this is so we ask why this is so, so also, when we know about something that it is simply, we then ask what it is, for example, 'what is God?' or 'what is man?' Therefore these, and this many, are the questions we ask, which, when we have answered them, we are said to know scientifically.

Then, when he says "Now when we ask..." he shows how to aforesaid questions are related to the middle. And concerning this he does three things: first, he proposes what he intends to do, second, he manifests what he said... third, he proves what he proposes. ...

About the first thing it must be said that of the four questions mentioned, of which two place into number and two do not, the first of each [group,] namely, the question whether it is so and the question whether it is, have something in common. And he says that when we ask about something whether this is that or when we ask whether it is simply, we seek nothing other than whether we can find some middle of that which we seek or not; which is not said according to the form of the question itself.

For when I ask whether the sun is eclipsed or whether man is, I do not ask from the very form of the question whether there is some middle through which it can be demonstrated either that the sun is eclipsed or that man is: but if the sun is eclipsed, or man is, it follows that it is possible to find some middle to demonstrate these things which are sought. For no question arises about immediate things, which, even if true, nevertheless do not have a middle; because things of this kind, since they are manifest, do not fall under question. Thus, then, whoever asks whether this is so or whether this is simply, asks, consequently, whether there is a middle for these things.

For in the question whether it is or that it is, whether that which is the middle is is sought; because that which is the middle is the reason for that about which it is asked whether this is so or whether this is simply, as will be said below. Therefore [the middle] is not sought under the notion of a middle.

Yet, having found what is sought through these two questions, one happens to know either that it is so or that it is; of which the latter is to know being simply, the former being in part, as when we know that man is white. ...

When, that it is so being known, we ask why it is so, and whether it is so being known, we ask what it is, we are then asking what the middle is. And, similarly, this must be taken, not according to the form of the question, but according to concomitance. For whoever seeks the cause on account of which the sun is eclipsed is not seeking that as demonstrating the middle, but he seeks that which the middle is: because it follows that, when this is found, he is able to demonstrate. Similarly with the question what it is. ...

Then, when he says "In all these..." he proves what he proposed, namely, that the aforesaid questions pertain to the middle. And first, he proves this through reason; secondly, he proves it through a sign.

He first concludes from what he has just manifested that in all the aforementioned questions, either whether there is a middle is sought, (namely, in the question whether it is so and in the question whether it is,) or what the middle is is sought (namely, in the question why it is so and in the question what it is.) And he proves that the question why seeks what the middle is.

For it is manifest that the cause is the middle in demonstration, which makes [someone] know; since to understand the cause of the thing is to know [scientifically]. But the cause is what is sought in all the aforesaid questions.

Which he first makes manifest in the question whether it is so. For when one asks whether the moon is eclipsed, it is asked in the manner explained above, whether something is the cause of the eclipse of the moon or not. And he next manifests this in the question why. For when we know that something is the cause of the eclipse of the moon, we ask what that cause is; and this is to ask why.

And the same notion is in the other questions, as he manifests through what follows. For he says that, whether we take some thing to be, not this or this, (for example, when I say 'man is white' or 'man is grammatical,') but we take the substance itself to be simply; or we do not take some substance to be simply, but [we take] a certain thing to be something, placing into number, (whether that thing is of the number of those which are predicated *per se*, or it is of the number of those which are predicated *per accidens*), whether we take the thing to be in this way or in that, its cause is the middle to demonstrating it.

He next explains what he said, 'that substance is, simply,' when we ask about the moon or the earth or a triangle or any subject whatsoever whether it is, and some middle is taken to demonstrate this. And I say that a thing is something, when we ask [whether there is] an eclipse concerning the moon, or equality or inequality concerning a triangle, or about the earth whether it is in the middle of the world or not. ...

Then, when he says, "That our question..." he shows what he proposed through a sensible sign. And he says that those things in which the middle is sensible manifestly show that every question is a question of the middle: namely, because when the middle is made known through sense, there is no room for a question. For then do we ask some one of the aforementioned questions among sensible things, when we do not sense the middle: just as we ask whether there is an eclipse of the moon or not, because we do not sense the middle which is the cause making the moon eclipsed. But if we were in that place which is above the moon, we would see how the moon is eclipsed by entering the shadow of the earth; and therefore we would ask nothing about this, neither whether it is or why; but at the same time each would be made manifest to us.

And because someone in objecting could say that the sense is of singular things, but those which are sought are universals, just as are those which are known [scientifically;] and thus it may not seem that is it possible for us to know that about which there is a question through sense: therefore, as if responding to this objection, he adds that from the very fact that we sense the particular, namely, that this body of the moon enters this shadow of the earth at that time, it immediately happens to us that we know the universal. For our sense would be about this, that the light of the sun is now obstructed through the opposition of the earth; and through this it would be manifest to us that the moon is now eclipsed. And because we ourselves conclude that the eclipse of the moon always comes about in this way, in our knowledge our sensing of the singular thing becomes universal immediately.

Thomas Aquinas, *Summa Theologica*, Ia

Treatise on Sacred Doctrine

Question One: The Nature and Extent of Sacred Doctrine

To place our purpose within proper limits, we first endeavor to investigate the nature and extent of this sacred doctrine. Concerning this there are ten points of inquiry:

(1) Whether it is necessary?
(2) Whether it is a science?
(3) Whether it is one or many?
(4) Whether it is speculative or practical?
(5) How it is compared with other sciences?
(6) Whether it is the same as wisdom?
(7) Whether God is its subject-matter?
(8) Whether it is a matter of argument?
(9) Whether it rightly employs metaphors and similes?
(10) Whether the Sacred Scripture of this doctrine may be expounded in different senses?

Article 1: Whether, besides philosophy, any further doctrine is required?

OBJ 1: It seems that, besides philosophical science, we have no need of any further knowledge. For man should not seek to know what is above reason: "Seek not the things that are too high for thee" (Ecclesiastes 3:22). But whatever is not above reason is fully treated of in philosophical science. Therefore any other knowledge besides philosophical science is superfluous.

OBJ 2: Further, knowledge can be concerned only with being, for nothing can be known, save what is true; and all that is, is true. But everything that is, is treated of in philosophical science---even God Himself; so that there is a part of philosophy called theology, or the divine science, as Aristotle has proved (De Metaphysica vi).

Therefore, besides philosophical science, there is no need of any further knowledge.

On the contrary, It is written (2 Timothy 3:16): "All Scripture, inspired of God is profitable to teach, to reprove, to correct, to instruct in justice." Now Scripture, inspired of God, is no part of philosophical science, which has been built up by human reason. Therefore it is useful that besides philosophical science, there should be other knowledge, i.e. inspired of God.

I answer that, It was necessary for man's salvation that there should be a knowledge revealed by God besides philosophical science built up by human reason. Firstly, indeed, because man is directed to God, as to an end that surpasses the grasp of his reason: "The eye hath not seen, O God, besides Thee, what things Thou hast prepared for them that wait for Thee" (Isaiah 66:4). But the end must first be known by men who are to direct their thoughts and actions to the end. Hence it was necessary for the salvation of man that certain truths which exceed human reason should be made known to him by divine revelation. Even as regards those truths about God which human reason could have discovered, it was necessary that man should be taught by a divine revelation; because the truth about God such as reason could discover, would only be known by a few, and that after a long time, and with the admixture of many errors. Whereas man's whole salvation, which is in God, depends upon the knowledge of this truth. Therefore, in order that the salvation of men might be brought about more fitly and more surely, it was necessary that they should be taught divine truths by divine revelation. It was therefore necessary that besides philosophical science built up by reason, there should be a sacred science learned through revelation.

Reply OBJ 1: Although those things which are beyond man's knowledge may not be sought for by man through his reason, nevertheless, once they are revealed by God, they must be accepted by faith. Hence the sacred text continues, "For many things are shown to thee above the understanding of man" (Ecclesiasticus 3:25). And in this, the sacred science consists.

Reply OBJ 2: Sciences are differentiated according to the various means through which knowledge is obtained. For the astronomer and the physicist both may prove the same conclusion: that the earth, for instance, is round: the astronomer by means of mathematics (i.e. abstracting from matter), but the physicist by means of matter itself. Hence there is no reason why those things which may be learned from philosophical science, so far as they can be known by natural reason, may not also be taught us by another science so far as they fall within revelation. Hence theology included in sacred doctrine differs in kind from that theology which is part of philosophy.

Article 8: Whether sacred doctrine is a matter of argument?

OBJ 1: It seems this doctrine is not a matter of argument. For Ambrose says (De Fide 1): "Put arguments aside where faith is sought." But in this doctrine, faith especially is sought: "But these things are written that you may believe" (John 20:31). Therefore sacred doctrine is not a matter of argument.

OBJ 2: Further, if it is a matter of argument, the argument is either from authority or from reason. If it is from authority, it seems unbefitting its dignity, for the proof from authority is the weakest form of proof. But if it is from reason, this is unbefitting its end, because, according to Gregory (Hom. 26), "faith has no merit in those things of which human reason brings its own experience." Therefore sacred doctrine is not a matter of argument.

On the contrary, The Scripture says that a bishop should "embrace that faithful word which is according to doctrine, that he may be able to exhort in sound doctrine and to convince the gainsayers" (Titus 1:9).

I answer that, As other sciences do not argue in proof of their principles, but argue from their principles to demonstrate other truths in these sciences: so this doctrine does not argue in proof of its principles, which are the articles of faith, but from them it goes on to prove something else; as the Apostle from the resurrection of Christ argues in proof of the general resurrection (1 Corinthians 15). However, it is to be borne in mind, in regard to the philosophical sciences, that the inferior sciences neither prove their principles nor dispute with those who deny them, but leave this to a higher science; whereas the highest of them, viz. metaphysics, can dispute with one who denies its principles, if only the opponent will make some concession; but if he concede nothing, it can have no dispute with him, though it can answer his objections. Hence Sacred Scripture, since it has no science above itself, can dispute with one who denies its principles only if the opponent admits some at least of the truths obtained through divine revelation; thus we can argue with heretics from texts in Holy Writ, and against those who deny one article of faith, we can argue from another. If our opponent believes nothing of divine revelation, there is no longer any means of proving the articles of faith by reasoning, but only of answering his objections—if he has any—against faith. Since faith rests upon infallible truth, and since the contrary of a truth can never be demonstrated, it is clear that the arguments brought against faith cannot be demonstrations, but are difficulties that can be answered.

Reply OBJ 1: Although arguments from human reason cannot avail to prove what must be received on faith, nevertheless, this doctrine argues from articles of faith to other truths.

Reply OBJ 2: This doctrine is especially based upon arguments from authority, inasmuch as its principles are obtained by revelation: thus we ought to believe on the authority of those to whom the revelation has been made. Nor does this take away from the dignity of this doctrine, for although the argument from authority based on human reason is the weakest, yet the argument from authority based on divine revelation is the strongest. But sacred doctrine makes use even of human reason, not, indeed, to prove faith (for thereby the merit of faith would come to an end), but to make clear other things that are put forward in this doctrine. Since therefore grace does not destroy nature but perfects it, natural reason should minister to faith as the natural bent of the will ministers to charity. Hence the Apostle says: "Bringing into captivity every understanding unto the obedience of Christ" (2 Corinthians 10:5). Hence sacred doctrine makes use also of the authority of philosophers in those questions in which they were able to know the truth by natural reason, as Paul quotes a saying of Aratus: "As some also of your own poets said: For we are also His offspring" (Acts 17:28). Nevertheless, sacred doctrine makes use of these authorities as extrinsic and probable arguments; but properly uses the authority of the canonical Scriptures as an incontrovertible proof, and the authority of the doctors of the Church as one that may properly be used, yet merely as probable. For our faith rests upon the revelation made to the apostles and prophets who wrote the canonical books, and not on the revelations (if any such there are) made to other doctors. Hence Augustine says (Ep. ad Hieron. xix,1): "Only those books of Scripture which are called canonical have I learned to hold in such honor as to believe their authors have not erred in any way in writing them. But other authors I so read as not to deem everything in their works to be true, merely on account of their having so thought and written, whatever may have been their holiness and learning."

Treatise on The One God

Question Two: The Existence of God

Because the chief aim of sacred doctrine is to teach the knowledge of God, not only as He is in Himself, but also as He is the beginning of things and their last end, and especially of rational creatures, as is clear from what has been already said, therefore, in our endeavor to expound this science, we shall treat: (1) Of God; (2) Of the rational creature's advance towards God; (3) Of Christ, Who as man, is our way to God.

In treating of God there will be a threefold division, for we shall consider: (1) Whatever concerns the Divine Essence; (2) Whatever concerns the distinctions of Persons; (3) Whatever concerns the procession of creatures from Him.

Concerning the Divine Essence, we must consider: (1) Whether God exists? (2) The manner of His existence, or, rather, what is not the manner of His existence; (3) Whatever concerns His operations—namely, His knowledge, will, power.

Concerning the first, there are three points of inquiry:

(1) Whether the proposition "God exists" is self-evident?
(2) Whether it is demonstrable?
(3) Whether God exists?

Article 1: Whether the existence of God is self-evident?

OBJ 1: It seems that the existence of God is self-evident. Now those things are said to be self-evident to us the knowledge of which is naturally implanted in us, as we can see in regard to first principles. But as Damascene says (De Fide Orthodoxa i,1, 3), "the knowledge of God is naturally implanted in all." Therefore the existence of God is self-evident.

OBJ 2: Further, those things are said to be self-evident which are known as soon as the terms are known, which the Philosopher (Analytica Posteriora i,3) says is true of the first principles of demonstration. Thus, when the nature of a whole and of a part is known, it is at once recognized that every whole is greater than its part. But as soon as the signification of the word God is understood, it is at once seen that God exists. For by this word is signified that thing than which nothing greater can be conceived. But that which exists actually and mentally is greater than that which exists only mentally. Therefore, since as soon as the word God is understood it exists mentally, it also follows that it exists actually. Therefore the proposition "God exists" is self-evident.

OBJ 3: Further, the existence of truth is self-evident. For whoever denies the existence of truth grants that truth does not exist: and, if truth does not exist, then the proposition "Truth does not exist" is true: and if there is anything true, there must be truth. But God is truth itself: "I am the way, the truth, and the life" (John 14:6) Therefore "God exists" is self-evident.

On the contrary, No one can mentally admit the opposite of what is self-evident; as the Philosopher (De Metaphysica iv,4) states concerning the first principles of demonstration. But the opposite of the proposition "God is" can be mentally admitted: "The fool said in his heart, There is no God" (Psalm 52:1). Therefore, that God exists is not self-evident.

I answer that, A thing can be self-evident in either of two ways: on the one hand, self-evident in itself, though not to us; on the other, self-evident in itself, and to us. A proposition is self-evident because the predicate is included in the essence of the subject, as "Man is an animal," for animal is contained in the essence of man. If, therefore the essence of the predicate and subject be known to all, the proposition will be self-evident to all; as is clear with regard to the first principles of demonstration, the terms of which are common things that no one is ignorant of, such as being and non-being, whole and part, and such like. If, however, there are some to whom the essence of the predicate and subject is unknown, the proposition will be self-evident in itself, but not to those who do not know the meaning of the predicate and subject of the proposition. Therefore, it happens, as Boethius says (De Hebdomadibus the title of which is: "Whether all that is, is good"), "that there are some mental concepts self-evident only to the learned, as that incorporeal substances are not in space." Therefore I say that this proposition, "God exists," of itself is self-evident, for the predicate is the same as the subject, because God is His own existence as will be hereafter shown (Q3,A4). Now because we do not know the essence of God, the proposition is not self-evident to us; but needs to be demonstrated by things that are more known to us, though less known in their nature---namely, by effects.

Reply OBJ 1: To know that God exists in a general and confused way is implanted in us by nature, inasmuch as God is man's beatitude. For man naturally desires happiness, and what is naturally desired by man must be naturally known to him. This, however, is not to know absolutely that God exists; just as to know that someone is approaching is not the same as to know that Peter is approaching, even though it is Peter who is approaching; for many there are who imagine that man's perfect good which is happiness, consists in riches, and others in pleasures, and others in something else.

Reply OBJ 2: Perhaps not everyone who hears this word God understands it to signify something than which nothing greater can be thought, seeing that some have believed God to be a body. Yet, granted that everyone understands that by this word God is signified something than which nothing greater can be thought, nevertheless, it does not therefore follow that he understands that what the word signifies exists actually, but only that it exists mentally. Nor can it be argued that it actually exists, unless it be admitted that there actually exists something than which nothing greater can be thought; and this precisely is not admitted by those who hold that God does not exist.

Reply OBJ 3: The existence of truth in general is self-evident but the existence of a Primal Truth is not self-evident to us.

Article 2: Whether it can be demonstrated that God exists?

OBJ 1: It seems that the existence of God cannot be demonstrated. For it is an article of faith that God exists. But what is of faith cannot be demonstrated, because a demonstration produces scientific knowledge; whereas faith is of the unseen (Hebrews 11:1). Therefore it cannot be demonstrated that God exists.

OBJ 2: Further, the essence is the middle term of demonstration. But we cannot know in what God's essence consists, but solely in what it does not consist; as Damascene says (De Fide Orthodoxa i,4). Therefore we cannot demonstrate that God exists.

OBJ 3: Further, if the existence of God were demonstrated, this could only be from His effects. But His effects are not proportionate to Him, since He is infinite and His effects are finite; and between the finite and infinite there is no proportion. Therefore, since a cause cannot be demonstrated by an effect not proportionate to it, it seems that the existence of God cannot be demonstrated.

On the contrary, The Apostle says: "The invisible things of Him are clearly seen, being understood by the things that are made" (Romans 1:20). But this would not be unless the existence of God could be demonstrated through the things that are made; for the first thing we must know of anything is whether it exists.

I answer that, Demonstration can be made in two ways: One is through the cause, and is called a priori, and this is to argue from what is prior absolutely. The other is through the effect, and is called a demonstration a posteriori; this is to argue from what is prior relatively only to us. When an effect is better known to us than its cause, from the effect we proceed to the knowledge of the cause. And from every effect the existence of its proper cause can be demonstrated, so long as its effects are better known to us; because since every effect depends upon its cause, if the effect exists, the cause must pre-exist. Hence the existence of God, in so far as it is not self-evident to us, can be demonstrated from those of His effects which are known to us.

Reply OBJ 1: The existence of God and other like truths about God, which can be known by natural reason, are not articles of faith, but are preambles to the articles; for faith presupposes natural knowledge, even as grace presupposes nature, and perfection supposes something that can be perfected. Nevertheless, there is nothing to prevent a man, who cannot grasp a proof, accepting, as a matter of faith, something which in itself is capable of being scientifically known and demonstrated.

Reply OBJ 2: When the existence of a cause is demonstrated from an effect, this effect takes the place of the definition of the cause in proof of the cause's existence. This is especially the case in regard to God, because, in order to prove the existence of anything, it is necessary to accept as a middle term the meaning of the word, and not its essence, for the question of its essence follows on the question of its existence. Now the names given to God are derived from His effects; consequently, in demonstrating the existence of God from His effects, we may take for the middle term the meaning of the word God.

Reply OBJ 3: From effects not proportionate to the cause no perfect knowledge of that cause can be obtained. Yet from every effect the existence of the cause can be clearly demonstrated, and so we can demonstrate the existence of God from His effects; though from them we cannot perfectly know God as He is in His essence.

Article 3: Whether God exists?

OBJ 1: It seems that God does not exist; because if one of two contraries be infinite, the other would be altogether destroyed. But the word God means that He is infinite goodness. If, therefore, God existed, there would be no evil discoverable; but there is evil in the world. Therefore God does not exist.

OBJ 2: Further, it is superfluous to suppose that what can be accounted for by a few principles has been produced by many. But it seems that everything we see in the world can be accounted for by other principles, supposing God did not exist. For all natural things can be reduced to one principle which is nature; and all voluntary things can be reduced to one principle which is human reason, or will. Therefore there is no need to suppose God's existence.

On the contrary, It is said in the person of God: "I am Who am." (Exodus 3:14)

I answer that, The existence of God can be proved in five ways.

The first and more manifest way is the argument from motion. It is certain, and evident to our senses, that in the world some things are in motion. Now whatever is in motion is put in motion by another, for nothing can be in motion except it is in potentiality to that towards which it is in motion; whereas a thing moves inasmuch as it is in act. For motion is nothing else than the reduction of something from potentiality to actuality. But nothing can be reduced from potentiality to actuality, except by something in a state of actuality. Thus that which is actually hot, as fire, makes wood, which is potentially hot, to be actually hot, and thereby moves and changes it. Now it is not possible that the same thing should be at once in actuality and potentiality in the same respect, but only in different respects. For what is actually hot cannot simultaneously be potentially hot; but it is simultaneously potentially cold. It is therefore impossible that in the same respect and in the same way a thing should be both mover and moved, i.e. that it should move itself. Therefore, whatever is in motion must be put in motion by another. If that by which it is put in motion be itself put in motion, then this also must needs be put in motion by another, and that by another again. But this cannot go on to infinity, because then there would be no first mover, and, consequently, no other mover; seeing that subsequent movers move only inasmuch as they are put in motion by the first mover; as the staff moves only because it is put in motion by the hand. Therefore it is necessary to arrive at a first mover, put in motion by no other; and this everyone understands to be God.

The second way is from the nature of the efficient cause. In the world of sense we find there is an order of efficient causes. There is no case known (neither is it, indeed, possible) in which a thing is found to be the efficient cause of itself; for so it would be prior to itself, which is impossible. Now in efficient causes it is not possible to go on to infinity, because in all efficient causes following in order, the first is the cause of the intermediate cause, and the intermediate is the cause of the ultimate cause, whether the intermediate cause be several, or only one. Now to take away the cause is to take away the effect. Therefore, if there be no first cause among efficient causes, there will be no ultimate, nor any intermediate cause. But if in efficient causes it is possible to go on to infinity, there will be no first efficient cause, neither will there be an ultimate effect, nor any intermediate efficient causes; all of which is plainly false. Therefore it is necessary to admit a first efficient cause, to which everyone gives the name of God.

The third way is taken from possibility and necessity, and runs thus. We find in nature things that are possible to be and not to be, since they are found to be generated, and to corrupt, and consequently, they are possible to be and not to be. But it is impossible for these always to exist, for that which is possible not to be at some time is not. Therefore, if everything is possible not to be, then at one time there could have been nothing in existence. Now if this were true, even now there would be nothing in existence, because that which does not exist only begins to exist by something already existing. Therefore, if at one time nothing was in existence, it would have been impossible for anything to have begun to exist; and thus even now nothing would be in existence---which is absurd. Therefore, not all beings are merely possible, but there must exist something the existence of which is necessary. But every necessary thing either has its necessity caused by another, or not. Now it is impossible to go on to infinity in necessary things which have their necessity caused by another, as has been already proved in regard to efficient causes. Therefore we cannot but postulate the existence of some being having of itself its own necessity, and not receiving it from another, but rather causing in others their necessity. This all men speak of as God.

The fourth way is taken from the gradation to be found in things. Among beings there are some more and some less good, true, noble and the like. But "more" and "less" are predicated of different things, according as they resemble in their different ways something which is the maximum, as a thing is said to be hotter according as it more nearly resembles that which is hottest; so that there is something which is truest, something best, something noblest and, consequently, something which is uttermost being; for those things that are greatest in truth are greatest in being, as it is written in <u>De Metaphysica</u> ii. Now the maximum in any genus is the cause of all in that genus; as fire, which is the maximum heat, is the cause of all hot things. Therefore there must also be something which is to all beings the cause of their being, goodness, and every other perfection; and this we call God.

The fifth way is taken from the governance of the world. We see that things which lack intelligence, such as natural bodies, act for an end, and this is evident from their acting always, or nearly always, in the same way, so as to obtain the best result. Hence it is plain that not fortuitously, but designedly, do they achieve their end. Now whatever lacks intelligence cannot move towards an end, unless it be directed by some being endowed with knowledge and intelligence; as the arrow is shot to its mark by the archer. Therefore some intelligent being exists by whom all natural things are directed to their end; and this being we call God.

Reply OBJ 1: As Augustine says (Enchiridion 11): "Since God is the highest good, He would not allow any evil to exist in His works, unless His omnipotence and goodness were such as to bring good even out of evil." This is part of the infinite goodness of God, that He should allow evil to exist, and out of it produce good.

Reply OBJ 2: Since nature works for a determinate end under the direction of a higher agent, whatever is done by nature must needs be traced back to God, as to its first cause. So also whatever is done voluntarily must also be traced back to some higher cause other than human reason or will, since these can change or fail; for all things that are changeable and capable of defect must be traced back to an immovable and self-necessary first principle, as was shown in the body of the Article.

Descartes, Meditations on First Philosophy: V

But now if because I can draw from my thought the idea of an object, it follows that all I clearly and distinctly apprehend to pertain to this object, does in truth belong to it, may I not from this derive an argument for the existence of God? It is certain that I no less find the idea of a God in my consciousness, that is the idea of a being supremely perfect, than that of any figure or number whatever: and I know with not less clearness and distinctness that an [actual and] eternal existence pertains to his nature than that all which is demonstrable of any figure or number really belongs to the nature of that figure or number; and, therefore, although all the conclusions of the preceding Meditations were false, the existence of God would pass with me for a truth at least as certain as I ever judged any truth of mathematics to be.

Indeed such a doctrine may at first sight appear to contain more sophistry than truth. For, as I have been accustomed in every other matter to distinguish between existence and essence, I easily believe that the existence can be separated from the essence of God, and that thus God may be conceived as not actually existing. But, nevertheless, when I think of it more attentively, it appears that the existence can no more be separated from the essence of God, than the idea of a mountain from that of a valley, or the equality of its three angles to two right angles, from the essence of a [rectilinear] triangle; so that it is not less impossible to conceive a God, that is, a being supremely perfect, to whom existence is wanting, or who is devoid of a certain perfection, than to conceive a mountain without a valley.

But though, in truth, I cannot conceive a God unless as existing, any more than I can a mountain without a valley, yet, just as it does not follow that there is any mountain in the world merely because I conceive a mountain with a valley, so likewise, though I conceive God as existing, it does not seem to follow on that account that God exists; for my thought imposes no necessity on things; and as I may imagine a winged horse, though there be none such, so I could perhaps attribute existence to God, though no God existed.

But the cases are not analogous, and a fallacy lurks under the semblance of this objection: for because I cannot conceive a mountain without a valley, it does not follow that there is any mountain or valley in existence, but simply that the mountain or valley, whether they do or do not exist, are inseparable from each other; whereas, on the other hand, because I cannot conceive God unless as existing, it follows that existence is inseparable from him, and therefore that he really exists: not that this is brought about by my thought, or that it imposes any necessity on things, but, on the contrary, the necessity which lies in the thing itself, that is, the necessity of the existence of God, determines me to think in this way: for it is not in my power to conceive a God without existence, that is, a being supremely perfect, and yet devoid of an absolute perfection, as I am free to imagine a horse with or without wings.

Blaise Pascal, *Pensées*, Section III

233. Infinite—nothing.—Our soul is cast into a body, where it finds number, dimension. Thereupon it reasons, and calls this nature necessity, and can believe nothing else.

Unity joined to infinity adds nothing to it, no more than one foot to an infinite measure. The finite is annihilated in the presence of the infinite, and becomes a pure nothing. So our spirit before God, so our justice before divine justice. There is not so great a disproportion between our justice and that of God as between unity and infinity.

The justice of God must be vast like His compassion. Now justice to the outcast is less vast and ought less to offend our feelings than mercy towards the elect.

We know that there is an infinite, and are ignorant of its nature. As we know it to be false that numbers are finite, it is therefore true that there is an infinity in number. But we do not know what it is. It is false that it is even, it is false that it is odd; for the addition of a unit can make no change in its nature. Yet it is a number, and every number is odd or even (this is certainly true of every finite number). So we may well know that there is a God without knowing what He is. Is there not one substantial truth, seeing there are so many things which are not the truth itself?

We know then the existence and nature of the finite, because we also are finite and have extension. We know the existence of the infinite and are ignorant of its nature, because it has extension like us, but not limits like us. But we know neither the existence nor the nature of God, because He has neither extension nor limits.

But by faith we know His existence; in glory we shall know His nature. Now, I have already shown that we may well know the existence of a thing, without knowing its nature.

Let us now speak according to natural lights.

If there is a God, He is infinitely incomprehensible, since, having neither parts nor limits, He has no affinity to us. We are then incapable of knowing either what He is or if He is. This being so, who will dare to undertake the decision of the question? Not we, who have no affinity to Him.

Who then will blame Christians for not being able to give a reason for their belief, since they profess a religion for which they cannot give a reason? They declare, in expounding it to the world, that it is a foolishness, stultitiam; and then you complain that they do not prove it! If they proved it, they would not keep their word; it is in lacking proofs that they are not lacking in sense. "Yes, but although this excuses those who offer it as such and takes away from them the blame of putting it forward without reason, it does not excuse those who receive it." Let us then examine this point, and say, "God is, or He is not." But to which side shall we incline? Reason can decide nothing here. There is an infinite chaos which separated us. A game is being played at the extremity of this infinite distance where heads or tails will turn up. What will you wager? According to reason, you can do neither the one thing nor the other; according to reason, you can defend neither of the propositions.

Do not, then, reprove for error those who have made a choice; for you know nothing about it. "No, but I blame them for having made, not this choice, but a choice; for again both he who chooses heads and he who chooses tails are equally at fault, they are both in the wrong. The true course is not to wager at all."

Yes; but you must wager. It is not optional. You are embarked. Which will you choose then? Let us see. Since you must choose, let us see which interests you least. You have two things to lose, the true and the good; and two things to stake, your reason and your will, your knowledge and your happiness; and your nature has two things to shun, error and misery. Your reason is no more shocked in choosing one rather than the other, since you must of necessity choose. This is one point settled. But your happiness? Let us weigh the gain and the loss in wagering that God is. Let us estimate these two chances. If you gain, you gain all; if you lose, you lose nothing. Wager, then, without hesitation that He is. "That is very fine. Yes, I must wager; but I may perhaps wager too much." Let us see. Since there is an equal risk of gain and of loss, if you had only to gain two lives, instead of one, you might still wager. But if there were three lives to gain, you would have to play (since you are under the necessity of playing), and you would be imprudent, when you are forced to play, not to chance your life to gain three at a game where there is an equal risk of loss and gain. But there is an eternity of life and happiness. And this being so, if there were an infinity of chances, of which one only would be for you, you would still be right in wagering one to win two, and you would act stupidly, being obliged to play, by refusing to stake one life against three at a game in which out of an infinity of chances there is one for you, if there were an infinity of an infinitely happy life to gain. But there is here an infinity of an infinitely happy life to gain, a chance of gain against a finite number of chances of loss, and what you stake is finite. It is all divided; where-ever the infinite is and there is not an infinity of chances of loss against that of gain, there is no time to hesitate, you must give all. And thus, when one is forced to play, he must renounce reason to preserve his life, rather than risk it for infinite gain, as likely to happen as the loss of nothingness.

For it is no use to say it is uncertain if we will gain, and it is certain that we risk, and that the infinite distance between the certainly of what is staked and the uncertainty of what will be gained, equals the finite good which is certainly staked against the uncertain infinite. It is not so, as every player stakes a certainty to gain an uncertainty, and yet he stakes a finite certainty to gain a finite uncertainty, without transgressing against reason. There is not an infinite distance between the certainty staked and the uncertainty of the gain; that is untrue. In truth, there is an infinity between the certainty of gain and the certainty of loss. But the uncertainty of the gain is proportioned to the certainty of the stake according to the proportion of the chances of gain and loss. Hence it comes that, if there are as many risks on one side as on the other, the course is to play even; and then the certainty of the stake is equal to the uncertainty of the gain, so far is it from fact that there is an infinite distance between them. And so our proposition is of infinite force, when there is the finite to stake in a game where there are equal risks of gain and of loss, and the infinite to gain. This is demonstrable; and if men are capable of any truths, this is one.

"I confess it, I admit it. But, still, is there no means of seeing the faces of the cards?" Yes, Scripture and the rest, etc. "Yes, but I have my hands tied and my mouth closed; I am forced to wager, and am not free. I am not released, and am so made that I cannot believe. What, then, would you have me do?"

True. But at least learn your inability to believe, since reason brings you to this, and yet you cannot believe. Endeavor, then, to convince yourself, not by increase of proofs of God, but by the abatement of your passions. You would like to attain faith and do not know the way; you would like to cure yourself of unbelief and ask the remedy for it. Learn of those who have been bound like you, and who now stake all their possessions. These are people who know the way which you would follow, and who are cured of an ill of which you would be cured. Follow the way by which they began; by acting as if they believed, taking the holy water, having masses said, etc. Even this will naturally make you believe, and deaden your acuteness. "But this is what I am afraid of." And why? What have you to lose?

But to show you that this leads you there, it is this which will lessen the passions, which are your stumbling-blocks.

The end of this discourse.—Now, what harm will befall you in taking this side? You will be faithful, humble, grateful, generous, a sincere friend, truthful. Certainly you will not have those poisonous pleasures, glory and luxury; but will you not have others? I will tell you that you will thereby gain in this life, and that, at each step you take on this road, you will see so great certainty of gain, so much nothingness in what you risk, that you will at last recognize that you have wagered for something certain and infinite, for which you have given nothing.

"Ah! This discourse transports me, charms me," etc.

If this discourse pleases you and seems impressive, know that it is made by a man who has knelt, both before and after it, in prayer to that Being, infinite and without parts, before whom he lays all he has, for you also to lay before Him all you have for your own good and for His glory, that so strength may be given to lowliness.

234. If we must not act save on a certainty, we ought not to act on religion, for it is not certain. But how many things we do on an uncertainty, sea voyages, battles! I say then we must do nothing at all, for nothing is certain, and that there is more certainty in religion than there is as to whether we may see to-morrow; for it is not certain that we may see to-morrow, and it is certainly possible that we may not, see it. We cannot say as much about religion. It is not certain that it is; but who will venture to say that it is certainly possible that it is not? Now when we work for to-morrow, and so on

an uncertainty, we act reasonably; for we ought to work for an uncertainty according to the doctrine of chance which was demonstrated above.

Saint Augustine has seen that we work for an uncertainty, on sea, in battle, etc. But he has not seen the doctrine of chance which proves that we should do so. Montaigne has seen that we are shocked at a fool, and that habit is all-powerful; but he has not seen the reason of this effect.

All these persons have seen the effects, but they have not seen the causes. They are, in comparison with those who have discovered the causes, as those who have only eyes are in comparison with those who have intellect. For the effects are perceptible by sense, and the causes are visible only to the intellect. And although these effects are seen by the mind, this mind is, in comparison with the mind which sees the causes, as the bodily senses are in comparison with the intellect.

John Locke, *Essay Concerning Human Understanding*: Book IV, Chapter 10: Of Our Knowledge of the Existence of a God

1. We are capable of knowing certainly that there is a God. Though God has given us no innate ideas of himself; though he has stamped no original characters on our minds, wherein we may read his being; yet having furnished us with those faculties our minds are endowed with, he hath not left himself without witness: since we have sense, perception, and reason, and cannot want a clear proof of him, as long as we carry ourselves about us. Nor can we justly complain of our ignorance in this great point; since he has so plentifully provided us with the means to discover and know him; so far as is necessary to the end of our being, and the great concernment of our happiness. But, though this be the most obvious truth that reason discovers, and though its evidence be (if I mistake not) equal to mathematical certainty: yet it requires thought and attention; and the mind must apply itself to a regular deduction of it from some part of our intuitive knowledge, or else we shall be as uncertain and ignorant of this as of other propositions, which are in themselves capable of clear demonstration. To show, therefore, that we are capable of knowing, i.e. being certain that there is a God, and how we may come by this certainty, I think we need go no further than ourselves, and that undoubted knowledge we have of our own existence.

2. For man knows that he himself exists. I think it is beyond question, that man has a clear idea of his own being; he knows certainly he exists, and that he is something. He that can doubt whether he be anything or no, I speak not to; no more than I would argue with pure nothing, or endeavor to convince nonentity that it were something. If any one pretends to be so skeptical as to deny his own existence, (for really to doubt of it is manifestly impossible,) let him for me enjoy his beloved happiness of being nothing, until hunger or some other pain convince him of the contrary. This, then, I think I may take for a truth, which every one's certain knowledge assures him of, beyond the liberty of doubting, viz. that he is something that actually exists.

3 He knows also that nothing cannot produce a being; therefore something must have existed from eternity. In the next place, man knows, by an intuitive certainty, that bare nothing can no more produce any real being, than it can be equal to two right angles. If a man knows not that nonentity, or the absence of all being, cannot be equal to two right angles, it is impossible he should know any demonstration in Euclid. If, therefore, we know there is some real being, and that nonentity cannot produce any real being, it is an evident demonstration, that from eternity there has been something; since what was not from eternity had a beginning; and what had a beginning must be produced by something else.

4. And that eternal Being must be most powerful. Next, it is evident, that what had its being and beginning from another, must also have all that which is in and belongs to its being from another too. All the powers it has must be owing to and received from the same source. This eternal source, then, of all being must also be the source and original of all power; and so this eternal Being must be also the most powerful.

5. And most knowing. Again, a man finds in himself perception and knowledge. We have then got one step further; and we are certain now that there is not only some being, but some knowing, intelligent being in the world. There was a time, then, when there was no knowing being, and when knowledge began to be; or else there has been also a knowing being from eternity. If it be said, there was a time when no being had any knowledge, when that eternal being was void of all understanding; I reply, that then it was impossible there should ever have been any knowledge: it being as impossible that things wholly void of knowledge, and operating blindly, and without any perception, should produce a knowing being, as it is impossible that a triangle should make itself three angles bigger than two right ones. For it is as repugnant to the idea of senseless matter, that it should put into itself sense, perception, and knowledge, as it is repugnant to the idea of a triangle, that it should put into itself greater angles than two right ones.

6. And therefore God. Thus, from the consideration of ourselves, and what we infallibly find in our own constitutions, our reason leads us to the knowledge of this certain and evident truth,- That there is an eternal, most powerful, and most knowing Being; which whether

any one will please to call God, it matters not. The thing is evident; and from this idea duly considered, will easily be deduced all those other attributes, which we ought to ascribe to this eternal Being. If, nevertheless, any one should be found so senselessly arrogant, as to suppose man alone knowing and wise, but yet the product of mere ignorance and chance; and that all the rest of the universe acted only by that blind haphazard; I shall leave with him that very rational and emphatical rebuke of Tully (I. ii. De Leg.), to be considered at his leisure: "What can be more sillily arrogant and misbecoming, than for a man to think that he has a mind and understanding in him, but yet in all the universe beside there is no such thing? Or that those things, which with the utmost stretch of his reason he can scarce comprehend, should be moved and managed without any reason at all?" *Quid est enim verius, quam neminem esse oportere tam stulte arrogantem, ut in se mentem et rationem putet inesse, in caelo mundoque non putet? Aut ea quae vix summa ingenii ratione comprehendat, nulla ratione moveri putet?*

From what has been said, it is plain to me we have a more certain knowledge of the existence of a God, than of anything our senses have not immediately discovered to us. Nay, I presume I may say, that we more certainly know that there is a God, than that there is anything else without us. When I say we know, I mean there is such a knowledge within our reach which we cannot miss, if we will but apply our minds to that, as we do to several other inquiries.

David Hume, Dialogues Concerning Natural Religion

PART 8

What you ascribe to the fertility of my invention, replied PHILO, is entirely owing to the nature of the subject. In subjects adapted to the narrow compass of human reason, there is commonly but one determination, which carries probability or conviction with it; and to a man of sound judgement, all other suppositions, but that one, appear entirely absurd and chimerical. But in such questions as the present, a hundred contradictory views may preserve a kind of imperfect analogy; and invention has here full scope to exert itself. Without any great effort of thought, I believe that I could, in an instant, propose other systems of cosmogony, which would have some faint appearance of truth, though it is a thousand, a million to one, if either yours or any one of mine be the true system.

For instance, what if I should revive the old EPICUREAN hypothesis? This is commonly, and I believe justly, esteemed the most absurd system that has yet been proposed; yet I know not whether, with a few alterations, it might not be brought to bear a faint appearance of probability. Instead of supposing matter infinite, as EPICURUS did, let us suppose it finite. A finite number of particles is only susceptible of finite transpositions: and it must happen, in an eternal duration, that every possible order or position must be tried an infinite number of times. This world, therefore, with all its events, even the most minute, has before been produced and destroyed, and will again be produced and destroyed, without any bounds and limitations. No one, who has a conception of the powers of infinite, in comparison of finite, will ever scruple this determination.

But this supposes, said DEMEA, that matter can acquire motion, without any voluntary agent or first mover.

And where is the difficulty, replied PHILO, of that supposition? Every event, before experience, is equally difficult and incomprehensible; and every event, after experience, is equally easy and intelligible. Motion, in many instances, from gravity, from elasticity, from electricity, begins in matter, without any known voluntary agent: and to suppose always, in these cases, an unknown voluntary agent, is mere hypothesis; and hypothesis attended with no advantages. The beginning of motion in matter itself is as conceivable a priori as its communication from mind and intelligence.

Besides, why may not motion have been propagated by impulse through all eternity, and the same stock of it, or nearly the same, be still upheld in the universe? As much is lost by the composition of motion, as much is gained by its resolution. And whatever the causes are, the fact is certain, that matter is, and always has been, in continual agitation, as far as human experience or tradition reaches. There is not probably, at present, in the whole universe, one particle of matter at absolute rest.

And this very consideration too, continued PHILO, which we have stumbled on in the course of the argument, suggests a new hypothesis of cosmogony, that is not absolutely absurd and improbable. Is there a system, an order, an economy of things, by which matter can preserve that perpetual agitation which seems essential to it, and yet maintain a constancy in the forms which it produces? There certainly is such an economy; for this is actually the case with the present world. The continual motion of matter, therefore, in less than infinite transpositions, must produce this economy or order; and by its very nature, that order, when once established, supports itself, for many ages, if not to eternity. But wherever matter is so poised, arranged, and adjusted, as to continue in perpetual motion, and yet preserve a constancy in the forms, its situation must, of necessity, have all the same appearance of art and contrivance which we observe at present. All the parts of each form must have a relation to each other, and to the whole; and the whole itself must have a relation to the other parts of the universe; to the element in which the form subsists; to the materials with which it repairs its waste and decay; and to every other form which is hostile or friendly. A defect in any of these particulars destroys the form; and the matter of which it is composed is again set loose, and is thrown into irregular motions and fermentations, till it unite itself to some other regular form. If no such form be prepared to receive it, and if there be a great quantity of this corrupted matter in the universe, the universe itself is entirely disordered; whether it be the feeble embryo of a world in its first beginnings that is thus destroyed, or the rotten carcass of one languishing in old age and infirmity. In either case, a chaos ensues; till finite, though innumerable revolutions produce at last some forms, whose parts and organs are so adjusted as to support the forms amidst a continued succession of matter.

Suppose (for we shall endeavour to vary the expression), that matter were thrown into any position, by a blind, unguided force; it is evident that this first position must, in all probability, be the most confused and most disorderly imaginable, without any resemblance to those works of human contrivance, which, along with a symmetry of parts, discover an adjustment of means to ends, and a tendency to self-preservation. If the actuating force cease after this operation, matter must remain for ever in disorder, and continue an immense chaos, without any proportion or activity. But suppose that the actuating force, whatever it be, still continues in matter, this first position will immediately give place to a second, which will likewise in all probability be as disorderly as the first, and so on through many successions of changes and revolutions. No particular order or position ever continues a moment unaltered. The original force, still remaining in activity, gives a perpetual restlessness to matter. Every possible situation is produced, and instantly destroyed. If a glimpse or dawn of order appears for a moment, it is instantly hurried away, and confounded, by that never-ceasing force which actuates every part of matter.

Thus the universe goes on for many ages in a continued succession of chaos and disorder. But is it not possible that it may settle at last, so as not to lose its motion and active force (for that we have supposed inherent in it), yet so as to preserve an uniformity of appearance, amidst the continual motion and fluctuation of its parts? This we find to be the case with the universe at present. Every individual is perpetually changing, and every part of every individual; and yet the whole remains, in appearance, the same. May we not hope for such a position, or rather be assured of it, from the eternal revolutions of unguided matter; and may not this account for all the appearing wisdom and contrivance which is in the universe? Let us contemplate the subject a little, and we shall find, that this adjustment, if attained by matter of a seeming stability in the forms, with a real and perpetual revolution or motion of parts, affords a plausible, if not a true solution of the difficulty.

It is in vain, therefore, to insist upon the uses of the parts in animals or vegetables, and their curious adjustment to each other. I would fain know, how an animal could subsist, unless its parts were so adjusted? Do we not find, that it immediately perishes whenever this adjustment ceases, and that its matter corrupting tries some new form? It happens indeed, that the parts of the world are so well adjusted, that some regular form immediately lays claim to this corrupted matter: and if it were not so, could the world subsist? Must it not dissolve as well as the animal, and pass through new positions and situations, till in great, but finite succession, it falls at last into the present or some such order?

It is well, replied CLEANTHES, you told us, that this hypothesis was suggested on a sudden, in the course of the argument. Had you had leisure to examine it, you would soon have perceived the insuperable objections to which it is exposed. No form, you say, can subsist, unless it possess those powers and organs requisite for its subsistence: some new order or economy must be tried, and so on, without intermission; till at last some order, which can support and maintain itself, is fallen upon. But according to this hypothesis, whence arise the many conveniences and advantages which men and all animals possess? Two eyes, two ears, are not absolutely necessary for the subsistence of the species. Human race might have been propagated and preserved, without horses, dogs, cows, sheep, and those innumerable fruits and products which serve to our satisfaction and enjoyment. If no camels had been created for the use of man in the sandy deserts of AFRICA and ARABIA, would the world have been dissolved? If no lodestone had been framed to give that wonderful and useful direction to the needle, would human society and the human kind have been immediately extinguished? Though the maxims of Nature be in general very frugal, yet instances of this kind are far from being rare; and any one of them is a sufficient proof of design, and of a benevolent design, which gave rise to the order and arrangement of the universe.

At least, you may safely infer, said PHILO, that the foregoing hypothesis is so far incomplete and imperfect, which I shall not scruple to allow. But can we ever reasonably expect greater success in any attempts of this nature? Or can we ever hope to erect a system of cosmogony, that will be liable to no exceptions, and will contain no circumstance repugnant to our limited and imperfect experience of the analogy of Nature? Your theory itself cannot surely pretend to any such advantage, even though you have run into Anthropomorphism, the better to preserve a conformity to common experience. Let us once more put it to trial. In all instances which we have ever seen, ideas are copied from real objects, and are ectypal, not archetypal, to express myself in learned terms: You reverse this order, and give thought the precedence. In all instances which we have ever seen, thought has no influence upon matter, except where that matter is so conjoined with it as to have an equal reciprocal influence upon it. No animal can move immediately any thing but the members of its own body; and indeed, the equality of action and reaction seems to be an universal law of nature: But your theory implies a contradiction to this experience. These instances, with many more, which it were easy to collect, (particularly the supposition of a mind or system of thought that is eternal, or, in other words, an animal ingenerable and immortal); these instances, I say, may teach all of us sobriety in condemning each other, and let us see, that as no system of this kind ought ever to be received from a slight analogy, so neither ought any to be rejected on account of a small incongruity. For that is an inconvenience from which we can justly pronounce no one to be exempted.

All religious systems, it is confessed, are subject to great and insuperable difficulties. Each disputant triumphs in his turn; while he carries on an offensive war, and exposes the absurdities, barbarities, and pernicious tenets of his antagonist. But all of them, on the whole, prepare a complete triumph for the Sceptic; who tells them, that no system ought ever to be embraced with regard to such subjects: For this plain reason, that no absurdity ought ever to be assented to with regard to any subject. A total suspense of judgement is here our only reasonable resource. And if every attack, as is commonly observed, and no defence, among Theologians, is successful; how complete must be his victory, who remains always, with all mankind, on the offensive, and has himself no fixed station or abiding city, which he is ever, on any occasion, obliged to defend?

Immanuel Kant, *Critique of Pure Reason:* Transcendental Dialectic, II, 3, §§ 4-7

Section IV. *Of the Impossibility of an Ontological Proof of the Existence of God*

[4] *Being* is evidently not a real predicate, or a concept of something that can be added to the concept of a thing. It is merely the admission of a thing, and of certain determinations in it. Logically, it is merely the copula of a judgment. The proposition, *God is almighty*, contains two concepts, each having its object, namely, God and almightiness. The small word *is*, is not an additional predicate, but only serves to put the predicate *in relation* to the subject. If, then, I take the subject (God) with all its predicates (including that of almightiness), and say, *God is*, or there is a God, I do not put a new predicate to the concept of God, but I only put the subject by itself, with all its predicates, in relation to my concept, as its object. Both must contain exactly the same kind of thing, and nothing can have been added to the concept, which expresses possibility only, by my thinking its object as simply given and saying, it is. And thus the real does not contain more than the possible. A hundred real dollars do not contain a penny more than a hundred possible dollars. For as the latter signify the concept, the former the object and its position by itself, it is clear that, in case the former contained more than the latter, my concept would not express the whole object, and would not therefore be its adequate concept. In my financial position no doubt there exists more by one hundred dollars, than by their concept only (that is their possibility), because in reality the object is not only contained analytically in my concept, but is added to my concept (which is a determination of my state), synthetically; but the conceived hundred dollars are not in the least increased through the existence which is outside my concept.

By whatever and by however many predicates I may think a thing (even in completely determining it), nothing is really added to it, if I add that the thing exists. Otherwise, it would not be the same that exists, but something more than was contained in the concept, and I could not say that the exact object of my concept existed. Nay, even if I were to think in a thing all reality, except one, that one missing reality would not be supplied by my saying that so defective a thing exists, but it would exist with the same defect with which I thought it; or what exists would be different from what I thought. If, then, I try to conceive a being, as the highest reality (without any defect), the question still remains, whether it exists or not. For though in my concept there may be wanting nothing of the possible real content of a thing in general, something is wanting in its relation to my whole state of thinking, namely, that the knowledge of that object should be possible *a posteriori* also. And here we perceive the cause of our difficulty. If we were concerned with an object of our senses, I could not mistake the existence of a thing for the mere concept of it; for by the concept the object is thought as only in harmony with the general conditions of a possible empirical knowledge, while by its existence it is thought as contained in the whole content of experience. Through this connection with the content of the whole experience, the concept of an object is not in the least increased; our thought has only received through it one more possible perception. If, however, we are thinking existence through the pure category alone, we need not wonder that we cannot find any characteristic to distinguish it from mere possibility.

Whatever, therefore, our concept of an object may contain, we must always step outside it, in order to attribute to it existence. With objects of the senses, this takes place through their connection with any one of my perceptions, according to empirical laws; with objects of pure thought, however, there is no means of knowing their existence, because it would have to be known entirely *a priori*, while our consciousness of every kind of existence, whether immediately by perception, or by conclusions which connect something with perception, belongs entirely to the field of experience, and any existence outside that field, though it cannot be declared to be absolutely impossible, is a presupposition that cannot be justified by anything.

The concept of a Supreme Being is, in many respects, a very useful idea, but being an idea only, it is quite incapable of increasing, by itself alone, our knowledge with regard to what exists, It cannot even do so much as to inform us any further as to its possibility. The analytical character of possibility, which consists in the absence of contradictions in mere positions (realities), cannot be denied to it; but the connection of all real properties in one and the same thing is a synthesis the possibility of which we cannot judge *a priori* because these realities are not given to us as such, and because, even if this were so, no judgment whatever takes place, it being necessary to look for the characteristic of the possibility of synthetical knowledge in experiences only, to which the object of an idea can never belong. Thus we see that the celebrated Leibniz is far from having achieved what he thought he had, namely, to understand *a priori* the possibility of so sublime an ideal Being.

Time and labor therefore are lost on the famous ontological (Cartesian) proof of the existence of a Supreme Being from mere concepts; and a man might as well imagine that he could become richer in knowledge by mere ideas, as a merchant in capital, if, in order to improve his position, he were to add a few noughts to his cash account.

SECTION V. *Of the Impossibility of a Cosmological Proof of the Existence of God*

[M. 486-7.] We shall now proceed to exhibit and to examine this cosmological proof which Leibniz calls also the proof *a contingentia mundi*.

It runs as follows: If there exists anything, there must exist an absolutely necessary Being also. Now I, at least, exist; therefore there exists an absolutely necessary Being. The minor contains an experience, the major the conclusion from experience in general to the existence of the necessary.[1] This proof therefore begins with experience, and is not entirely *a priori*, or ontological; and, as the object of all possible experience is called the world, this proof is called the *cosmological proof*. As it takes no account of any peculiar property of the objects of experience, by which this world of ours may differ from any other possible world, it is distinguished, in its name also,

---

[1] This conclusion is too well known to require detailed exposition. It rests on the apparently transcendental law of causality in nature, that everything contingent has its cause, which, if contingent again, must likewise have a cause, till the series of subordinate causes ends in an absolutely necessary cause, without which it could not be complete.

from the physico-theological proof, which employs as arguments, observations of the peculiar property of this our world of sense.

The proof then proceeds as follows: The necessary Being can be determined in one way only, that is, by one only of all possible opposite predicates; it must therefore be determined completely by its own concept. Now, there is only one concept of a thing possible, which *a priori* completely determines it, namely, that of the *ens realissimum*. It follows, therefore, that the concept of the *ens realissimum* is the only one by which a necessary Being can be thought, and therefore it is concluded that a highest Being exists by necessity.

There are so many sophistical propositions in this cosmological argument, that it really seems as if speculative reason had spent all her dialectical skill in order to produce the greatest possible transcendental illusion. Before examining it, we shall draw up a list of them, by which reason has put forward an old argument disguised as a new one, in order to appeal to the agreement of two witnesses, one supplied by pure reason, the other by experience, while in reality there is only one, namely, the first, which changes his dress and voice in order to be taken for a second. In order to have a secure foundation, this proof takes its stand on experience, and pretends to be different from the ontological proof, which places its whole confidence in pure concepts *a priori* only. The cosmological proof, however, uses that experience only in order to make one step, namely, to the existence of a necessary Being in general. What properties that Being may have, can never be learnt from the empirical argument, and for that purpose reason takes leave of it altogether, and tries to find out, from among concepts only, what properties an absolutely necessary Being ought to possess, i.e. which among all possible things contains in itself the requisite conditions (*requisita*) of absolute necessity. This requisite is believed by reason to exist in the concept of an *ens realissimum* only, and reason concludes at once that this must be the absolutely necessary Being. In this conclusion it is simply assumed that the concept of a being of the highest reality is perfectly adequate to the concept of absolute necessity in existence; so that the latter might be concluded from the former. This is the same proposition as that maintained in the ontological argument, and is simply taken over into the cosmological proof, nay, made its foundation, although the intention was to avoid it. For it is clear that absolute necessity is an existence from mere concepts. If, then, I say that the concept of the *ens realissimum* is such a concept, and is the only concept adequate to necessary existence, I am bound to admit that the latter may be deduced from the former. The whole conclusive strength of the so-called cosmological proof rests therefore in reality on the ontological proof from mere concepts, while the appeal to experience is quite superfluous, and, though it may lead us on to the concept of absolute necessity, it cannot demonstrate it with any definite object. For as soon as we intend to do this, we must at once abandon all experience, and try to find out which among the bare concepts may contain the conditions of the possibility of an absolutely necessary Being. But if in this way the possibility of such a Being has been perceived, its existence also has been proved: for what we are really saying is this, that under all possible things there is one which carries with it absolute necessity, or that this Being exists with absolute necessity... [M. 490]

We thus see that the second road taken by speculative reason, in order to prove the existence of the highest Being, is not only as illusory as the first, but commits in addition an *ignoratio elenchi*, promising to lead us by a new path, but after a short circuit bringing us back to the old one, which we had abandoned for its sake.

I said before that a whole nest of dialectical assumptions was hidden in that cosmological proof, and that transcendental criticism might easily detect and destroy it. I shall here enumerate them only, leaving it to the experience of the reader to follow up the fallacies and remove them.

We find, first, the transcendental principle of inferring a cause from the accidental. This principle, that everything contingent must have a cause, is valid in the world of sense only, and has not even a meaning outside it. For the purely intellectual concept of the contingent cannot produce a synthetical proposition like that of causality, and the principle of causality has no meaning and no criterion of its use, except in the world of sense, while here it is meant to help us beyond the world of sense.

Secondly. The inference of a first cause, based on the impossibility of an infinite ascending series of given causes in this world of sense—an inference which the principles of the use of reason do not allow us to draw even in experience, while here we extend that principle beyond experience, whither that series can never be prolonged.

Thirdly. The false self-satisfaction of reason with regard to the completion of that series, brought about by removing in the end every kind of condition, without which, nevertheless, no concept of necessity is possible, and by then, when any, definite concepts have become impossible, accepting this as a completion of our concept.

Fourthly. The mistaking the logical possibility of a concept of all united reality (without any internal contradiction) for the transcendental, which requires a principle for the practicability of such a synthesis, such principle however being applicable to the field of possible experience only, etc... [M. 492-3]

It may be allowable to admit the existence of a Being entirely sufficient to serve as the cause of all possible effects, simply in order to assist reason in her search for unity of causes. But to go so far as to say that *such a Being exists necessarily*, is no longer the modest language of an admissible hypothesis, but the bold assurance of apodictic certainty; for the knowledge of that which is absolutely necessary must itself possess absolute necessity... [M. 493-4]

Discovery and Explanation of the Dialectical Illusion in all Transcendental Proofs of the Existence of a Necessary Being

Both proofs, hitherto attempted, were transcendental, that is, independent of empirical principles. For although the cosmological proof assumes for its foundation an experience in general, it does not rest on any particular quality of it, but on pure principles of reason, with reference to an existence given by the empirical consciousness in general, and abandons even that guidance in order to derive its support from pure concepts only. What then in these transcendental proofs is the cause of the dialectical, but natural, illusion which connects the concepts of necessity and of the highest reality, and realizes and hypostasizes that which can only be an idea? What is the cause that renders it inevitable to admit something as necessary in itself among existing things, and yet makes us shrink back from the existence of such a Being as from an abyss? What is to be done that reason should understand itself on this point, and, escaping from the wavering state of hesitatingly approving or disapproving, acquire a calm insight into the matter? ... [M. 495-6]

If, therefore, I am obliged to think something necessary for all existing things, and at the same time am not justified in thinking of anything as in itself necessary, the conclusion is inevitable: that necessity and contingency do not concern things themselves, for otherwise there would be a contradiction, and that therefore neither of the two principles can be objective; but that they may possibly be subjective principles of reason only, according to which, on one side, we have to find for all that is given as existing, something that is necessary, and thus never to stop except when we have reached an *a priori* complete explanation; while on the other we must never hope for that completion, that is, never admit anything empirical as unconditioned, and thus dispense with its further derivation. In that sense both principles as purely heuristic and *regulative*, and affecting the formal interests of reason only, may well stand side by side. For the one tells us that we ought to philosophize on nature as if there was a necessary first cause for everything that exists, if only in order to introduce systematical unity into our knowledge, by always looking for such an idea as an imagined highest cause. The other warns us against mistaking any single determination concerning the existence of things for such a highest cause, i.e. for something absolutely necessary, and bids us to keep the way always open for further derivation, and to treat it always as conditioned. If, then, everything that is perceived in things has to be considered by us as only conditionally necessary, nothing that is empirically given can ever be considered as absolutely necessary.

It follows from this that the absolutely necessary must be accepted as *outside the world*, because it is only meant to serve as a principle of the greatest possible unity of phenomena, of which it is the highest cause, and that it can never be reached *in the world*, because the second rule bids you always to consider all empirical causes of that unity as derived... [M. 497-8]

The ideal of the Supreme Being is therefore, according to these remarks, nothing but a *regulative principle* of reason, which obliges us to consider all connection in the world as if it arose from an all-sufficient necessary cause, in order to found on it the rule of a systematical unity necessary according to general laws for the explanation of the world; it does not involve the assertion of an existence necessary by itself. It is impossible, however, at the same time, to escape from a transcendental *subreptio*, which leads us to represent that formal principle as constitutive, and to think that unity as hypostasized. It is the same with space. Space, though it is only a principle of sensibility, yet serves originally to make all forms possible, these being only limitations of it. For that very reason, however, it is mistaken for something absolutely necessary and independent, nay, for an object *a priori* existing in itself. It is the same here, and as this systematical unity of nature can in no wise become the principle of the empirical use of our reason, unless we base it on the idea of an *ens realissimum* as the highest cause, it happens quite naturally that we thus represent that idea as a real object, and that object again, as it is the highest condition, as necessary. Thus a *regulative* principle has been changed into a *constitutive* principle, which substitution becomes evident at once because, as soon as I consider that highest Being, which with regard to the world was absolutely (unconditionally) necessary, as a thing by itself, that necessity cannot be conceived, and can therefore have existed in my reason as a formal condition of thought only, and not as a material and substantial condition of existence.

SECTION VI. *Of the Impossibility of the Physico-theological Proof*

[M. 499-500] This present world presents to us so immeasurable a stage of variety, order, fitness, and beauty, whether we follow it up in the infinity of space or in its unlimited division, that even with the little knowledge which our poor understanding has been able to gather, all language, with regard to so many and inconceivable wonders, loses its vigor, all numbers their power of measuring, and all our thoughts their necessary determination; so that our judgment of the whole is lost in a speechless, but all the more eloquent astonishment. Everywhere we see a chain of causes and effects, of means and ends, of order in birth and death, and as nothing has entered by itself into the state in which we find it, all points to another thing as its cause. As that cause necessitates the same further inquiry, the whole universe would thus be lost in the abyss of nothing, unless we admitted something which, existing by itself, original and independent, outside the chain of infinite contingencies, should support it, and, as the cause of its origin, secure to it at the same time its permanence. Looking at all the things in the world, what greatness shall we attribute to that highest cause? We do not know the whole contents of the world, still less can we measure its magnitude by a comparison with all that is possible. But, as with regard to causality, we cannot do without a last and highest Being, why should we not fix the degree of its perfection *beyond everything else that is possible*? This we can easily do, though only in the faint outline of an abstract concept, if we represent to ourselves all possible perfections united in it as in one substance. Such a concept would agree with the demand of our reason, which requires parsimony in the number of principles; it would have no contradictions in itself, would be favorable to the extension of the employment of reason in the midst of experience, by guiding it towards order and system, and lastly, would never be decidedly opposed to any experience.

This proof will always deserve to be treated with respect. It is the oldest, the clearest, and most in conformity with human reason. It gives life to the study of nature, deriving its own existence from it, and thus constantly acquiring new vigor.

It reveals aims and intention, where our own observation would not by itself have discovered them, and enlarges our knowledge of nature by leading us towards that peculiar unity the principle of which exists outside nature. This knowledge reacts again on its cause, namely, the transcendental idea, and thus increases the belief in a supreme Author to an irresistible conviction.

It would therefore be not only extremely sad, but utterly vain to attempt to diminish the authority of that proof. Reason, constantly strengthened by the powerful arguments that come to hand by themselves, though they are no doubt empirical only, cannot be discouraged by any doubts of subtle and abstract speculation. Roused from every inquisitive indecision, as from a dream, by one glance at the wonders of nature and the majesty of the cosmos, reason soars from height to height till it reaches the highest, from the conditioned to conditions, till it reaches the supreme and unconditioned Author of all.

But although we have nothing to say against the reasonableness and utility of this line of argument, but wish, on the contrary, to commend and encourage it, we cannot approve of the claims which this proof advances to apodictic certainty, and to an approval on its own merits, requiring no favor, and no help from any other quarter. It cannot injure the good cause, if the dogmatical language of the overweening sophist is toned down to the moderate and modest statements of a faith which does not require unconditioned submission, yet is sufficient to give rest and comfort. I therefore maintain that the physico-theological proof can never establish by itself alone the existence of a Supreme Being, but must always leave it to the ontological proof (to which it serves only as an introduction), to supply its deficiency; so that, after all, it is the ontological proof which contains the *only possible argument* (supposing always that any speculative proof is possible), and human reason can never do without it.

The principal points of the physico-theological proof are the following. 1st. There are everywhere in the world clear indications of an intentional arrangement carried out with great wisdom, and forming a whole indescribably varied in its contents and infinite in extent.

2ndly. The fitness of this arrangement is entirely foreign to the things existing in the world, and belongs to them contingently only; that is, the nature of different things could never spontaneously, by the combination of so many means, cooperate towards definite aims, if these means had not been selected and arranged on purpose by a rational disposing principle, according to certain fundamental ideas.

3rdly. There exists, therefore, a sublime and wise cause (or many), which must be the cause of the world, not only as a blind and all-powerful nature, by means of unconscious *fecundity*, but as an intelligence, by *freedom*.

4thly. The unity of that cause may be inferred with certainty from the unity of the reciprocal relation of the parts of the world, as portions of a skillful edifice, so far as our experience reaches, and beyond it, with plausibility, according to the principles of analogy.

Without wishing to argue, for the sake of argument only, with natural reason, as to its conclusion in inferring from the analogy of certain products of nature with the works of human art, in which man does violence to nature, and forces it not to follow its own aims, but to adapt itself to ours (that is, from the similarity of certain products of nature with houses, ships, and watches), in inferring from this, I say, that a similar causality, namely, understanding and will, must be at the bottom of nature, and in deriving the internal possibility of a freely acting nature (which, it may be, renders all human art and even human reason possible) from another though superhuman art—a kind of reasoning, which probably could not stand the severest test of transcendental criticism; we are willing to admit, nevertheless, that if we have to name such a cause, we cannot do better than to follow the analogy of such products of human design, which are the only ones of which we know completely both cause and effect. There would be no excuse, if reason were to surrender a causality which it knows, and have recourse to obscure and indemonstrable principles of explanation, which it does not know.

According to this argument, the fitness and harmony existing in so many works of nature might prove the contingency of the form, but not of the matter, that is, the substance in the world, because, for the latter purpose, it would be necessary to prove in addition, that the things of the world were in themselves incapable of such order and harmony, according to general laws, unless there existed, even in their *substance*, the product of a supreme wisdom. For this purpose, very different arguments would be required from those derived from the analogy of human art. The utmost, therefore, that could be established by such a proof would be an *architect of the world*, always very much hampered by the quality of the material with which he has to work, not a *creator*, to whose idea everything is subject. This would by no means suffice for the purposed aim of proving an all-sufficient original Being. If we wished to prove the contingency of matter itself, we must have recourse to a transcendental argument, and this is the very thing which was to be avoided.

The inference, therefore, really proceeds from the order and design that can everywhere be observed in the world, as an entirely contingent arrangement, to the existence of a cause, *proportionate to it*. The concept of that cause must therefore teach us something quite *definite* about it, and can therefore be no other concept but that of a Being which possesses all might, wisdom, etc., in one word, all perfection of an all-sufficient Being. The predicates of a *very great*, of an astounding, of an immeasurable might and virtue give us no definite concept, and never tell us really what the thing is by itself. They are only relative representations of the magnitude of an object, which the observer (of the world) compares with himself and his own power of comprehension, and which would be equally grand, whether we magnify the object, or reduce the observing subject to smaller proportions in reference to it. Where we are concerned with the magnitude (of the perfection) of a thing in general, there exists no definite concept, except that which comprehends all possible perfection, and only the all (*omnitudo*) of reality is thoroughly determined in the concept.

Now I hope that no one would dare to comprehend the relation of that part of the world which he has observed (in its extent as well as in its contents) to omnipotence, the relation of the order of the world to the highest wisdom, and the relation of the unity of the world to the absolute unity of its author, etc. Physico-theology, therefore, can never give a definite concept of the highest cause of the world, and is insufficient, therefore, as a principle of theology, which is itself to form the basis of religion.

The step leading to absolute totality is entirely impossible on the empirical road. Nevertheless, that step is taken in the physico-theological proof. How then has this broad abyss been bridged over?

The fact is that, after having reached the stage of admiration of the greatness, the wisdom, the power, etc. of the Author of the world, and seeing no further advance possible, one suddenly leaves the argument carried on by empirical proofs, and lays hold of that contingency which, from the very first, was inferred from the order and design of the world. The next step from that contingency leads, by means of transcendental concepts only, to the existence of something absolutely necessary, and another step from the absolute necessity of the first cause to its completely determined or determining concept, namely, that of an all-embracing reality. Thus we see that the physico-tlheological proof, baffled in its own undertaking, takes suddenly refuge in the cosmological proof, and as this is only the ontological proof in disguise, it really carries out its original intention by means of pure reason only; though it so strongly disclaimed in the beginning all connection with it, and professed to base everything on clear proofs from experience... [M. 506-7]

Thus we have seen that the physico-theological proof rests on the cosmological, and the cosmological on the ontological proof of the existence of one original Being as the Supreme Being; and, as besides these three, there is no other path open to speculative reason, the ontological proof, based exclusively on pure concepts of reason, is the only possible one, always supposing that any proof of a proposition, so far transcending the empirical use of the understanding, is possible at all.

SECTION VII. *Criticism of all Theology based on Speculative Principles of Reason*

... [M. 508-13] If people, however, should prefer to call in question all the former proofs of the Analytic, rather than allow themselves to be robbed of their persuasion of the value of the proofs on which they have rested so long, they surely cannot decline my request, when I ask them to justify themselves, at least on this point, in what manner, and by what kind of illumination they trust themselves to soar above all possible experience, on the wings of pure ideas. I must ask to be excused from listening to new proofs, or to the tinkered workmanship of the old. No doubt the choice is not great, for all speculative proofs end in the one, namely, the ontological; nor need I fear to be much troubled by the inventive fertility of the dogmatical defenders of that reason which they have delivered from the bondage of the senses; nor should I even, without considering myself a very formidable antagonist, decline the challenge to detect the fallacy in every one of their attempts, and thus to dispose of their pretensions. But I know too well that the hope of better success will never be surrendered by those who have once accustomed themselves to dogmatical persuasion, and I therefore restrict myself to the one just demand, that my opponents should explain in general, from the nature of the human understanding, or from any other sources of knowledge, what we are to do in order to extend our knowledge entirely *a priori*, and to carry it to a point where no possible experience, and therefore no means whatever, is able to secure to a concept invented by ourselves its objective reality. In whatever way the understanding may have reached that concept, it is clearly impossible that the *existence* of its object could be found in it through analysis, because the very knowledge of the existence of the object implies that it exists *outside our thoughts*. We cannot in fact go beyond concepts, nor, unless we follow the empirical connection by which nothing but phenomena can be given, hope to discover new objects and imaginary beings.

Although then reason, in its purely speculative application, is utterly insufficient for this great undertaking, namely, to prove the existence of a Supreme Being, it has nevertheless this great advantage of being able to *correct* our knowledge of it, if it can be acquired from elsewhere, to make it consistent with itself and every intelligible view, and to purify it from everything incompatible with the concept of an original Being, and from all admixture of empirical limitations.

In spite of its insufficiency, therefore, transcendental theology has a very important negative use, as a constant test of our reason, when occupied with pure ideas only, which, as such, admit of a transcendental standard only. For suppose that on practical grounds the *admission* of a highest and all-sufficient Being, as the highest intelligence, were to maintain its validity without contradiction, it would be of the greatest importance that we should be able to determine that concept accurately on its transcendental side, as the concept of a necessary and most real Being, to remove from it what is contradictory to that highest reality and purely phenomenal (anthropomorphic in the widest sense), and at the same time to put an end to all opposite assertions, whether *atheistic, deistic,* or *anthropomorphistic.* Such a critical treatment would not be difficult, because the same arguments by which the insufficiency of human reason in asserting the existence of such a Being has been proved, must be sufficient also to prove the invalidity of opposite assertions. For whence can anybody, through pure speculation of reason, derive his knowledge that there is no Supreme Being, as the cause of all that exists, or that it can claim none of those qualities which we, to judge from their effects, represent to ourselves as compatible with the dynamical realties of a thinking Being, or that, in the latter case, they would be subject to all those limitations which sensibility imposes inevitably on all the intelligences known to us by experience?

For the purely speculative use of reason, therefore, the Supreme Being remains, no doubt, an ideal only, but an ideal *without a flaw*, a concept which finishes and crowns the whole of human knowledge, and the objective reality of which, though it cannot be proved, can neither be disproved in that way. If then there should be an Ethico-theology to supply that deficiency, transcendental theology, which before was problematical only, would prove itself indispensable in determining its concept, and in constantly testing reason, which is so often deceived by sensibility, and not even always in harmony with its own ideas. Necessity, infinity, unity, extramundane existence (not as a world-soul), eternity, free from conditions of time, omnipresence, free from conditions of space, omnipotence, etc., all these are transcendental predicates, and their purified concepts, which are so much required for every theology, can therefore be derived from transcendental theology only.

William Paley, *Natural Theology; or Evidences of the Existence and Attributes of the Deity*

NATURAL THEOLOGY.

CHAPTER I. STATE OF THE ARGUMENT.

In crossing a heath, suppose I pitched my foot against a stone, and were asked how the stone came to be there; I might possibly answer, that, for any thing I knew to the contrary, it had lain there for ever: nor would it perhaps be very easy to show the absurdity of this answer. But suppose I had found a watch upon the ground, and it should be inquired how the watch happened to be in that place; I should hardly think of the answer which I had before given, that, for any thing I knew, the watch might have always been there. Yet why should not this answer serve for the watch as well as for the stone? why is it not as admissible in the second case, as in the first? For this reason, and for no other, viz. that, when we come to inspect the watch, we perceive (what we could not discover in the stone) that its several parts are framed and put together for a purpose, e. g. that they are so formed and adjusted as to produce motion, and that motion so regulated as to point out the hour of the day; that, if the different parts had been differently shaped from what they are, of a different size from what they are, or placed after any other manner, or in any other order, than that in which they are placed, either no motion at all would have been carried on in the machine, or none which would have answered the use that is now served by it. To reckon up a few of the plainest of these parts, and of their offices, all tending to one result:— We see a cylindrical box containing a coiled elastic spring, which, by its endeavour to relax itself, turns round the box. We next observe a flexible chain (artificially wrought for the sake of flexure), communicating the action of the spring from the box to the fusee. We then find a series of wheels, the teeth of which catch in, and apply to, each other, conducting the motion from the fusee to the balance, and from the balance to the pointer; and at the same time, by the size and shape of those wheels, so regulating that motion, as to terminate in causing an index, by an equable and measured progression, to pass over a given space in a given time. We take notice that the wheels are made of brass in order to keep them from rust; the springs of steel, no other metal being so elastic; that over the face of the watch there is placed a glass, a material employed in no other part of the work, but in the room of which, if there had been any other than a transparent substance, the hour could not be seen without opening the case. This mechanism being observed (it requires indeed an examination of the instrument, and perhaps some previous knowledge of the subject, to perceive and understand it; but being once, as we have said, observed and understood), the inference, we think, is inevitable, that the watch must have had a maker: that there must have existed, at some time, and at some place or other, an artificer or artificers who formed it for the purpose which we find it actually to answer; who comprehended its construction, and designed its use.

I. Nor would it, I apprehend, weaken the conclusion, that we had never seen a watch made; that we had never known an artist capable of making one; that we were altogether incapable of executing such a piece of workmanship ourselves, or of understanding in what manner it was performed; all this being no more than what is true of some exquisite remains of ancient art, of some lost arts, and, to the generality of mankind, of the more curious productions of modern manufacture. Does one man in a million know how oval frames are turned? Ignorance of this kind exalts our opinion of the unseen and unknown artist's skill, if he be unseen and unknown, but raises no doubt in our minds of the existence and agency of such an artist, at some former time, and in some place or other. Nor can I perceive that it varies at all the inference, whether the question arise concerning a human agent, or concerning an agent of a different species, or an agent possessing, in some respects, a different nature.

II. Neither, secondly, would it invalidate our conclusion, that the watch sometimes went wrong, or that it seldom went exactly right. The purpose of the machinery, the design, and the designer, might be evident, and in the case supposed would be evident, in whatever way we accounted for the irregularity of the movement, or whether we could account for it or not. It is not necessary that a machine be perfect, in order to show with what design it was made: still less necessary, where the only question is, whether it were made with any design at all.

III. Nor, thirdly, would it bring any uncertainty into the argument, if there were a few parts of the watch, concerning which we could not discover, or had not yet discovered, in what manner they conduced to the general effect; or even some parts, concerning which we could not ascertain, whether they conduced to that effect in any manner whatever. For, as to the first branch of the case; if by the loss, or disorder, or decay of the parts in question, the movement of the watch were found in fact to be stopped, or disturbed, or retarded, no doubt would remain in our minds as to the utility or intention of these parts, although we should be unable to investigate the manner according to which, or the connexion by which, the ultimate effect depended upon their action or assistance; and the more complex is the machine, the more likely is this obscurity to arise. Then, as to the second thing supposed, namely, that there were parts which might be spared, without prejudice to the movement of the watch, and that we had proved this by experiment,—these superfluous parts, even if we were completely assured that they were such, would not vacate the reasoning which we had instituted concerning other parts. The indication of contrivance remained, with respect to them, nearly as it was before.

IV. Nor, fourthly, would any man in his senses think the existence of the watch, with its various machinery, accounted for, by being told that it was one out of possible combinations of material forms; that whatever he had found in the place where he found the watch, must have contained some internal configuration or other; and that this configuration might be the structure now exhibited, viz. of the works of a watch, as well as a different structure.

V. Nor, fifthly, would it yield his inquiry more satisfaction to be answered, that there existed in things a principle of order, which had disposed the parts of the watch into their present form and situation. He never knew a watch made by the principle of order; nor can he even form to himself an idea of what is meant by a principle of order, distinct from the intelligence of the watch-maker.

VI. Sixthly, he would be surprised to hear that the mechanism of the watch was no proof of contrivance, only a motive to induce the mind to think so:

VII. And not less surprised to be informed, that the watch in his hand was nothing more than the result of the laws of metallicnature. It is a perversion of language to assign any law, as the efficient, operative cause of any thing. A law presupposes an agent; for it is only the mode, according to which an agent proceeds: it implies a power; for it is the order, according to which that power acts. Without this agent, without this power, which are both distinct from itself, the law does nothing; is nothing. The expression, the law of metallic nature, may sound strange and harsh to a philosophic ear; but it seems quite as justifiable as some others which are more familiar to him, such as the law of vegetable nature, the law of animal nature, or indeed as the law of nature in general, when assigned as the cause of phænomena, in exclusion of agency and power; or when it is substituted into the place of these.

VIII. Neither, lastly, would our observer be driven out of his conclusion, or from his confidence in its truth, by being told that he knew nothing at all about the matter. He knows enough for his argument: he knows the utility of the end: he knows the subserviency and adaptation of the means to the end. These points being known, his ignorance of other points, his doubts concerning other points, affect not the certainty of his reasoning. The consciousness of knowing little, need not beget a distrust of that which he does know.

CHAPTER II. STATE OF THE ARGUMENT CONTINUED.

SUPPOSE, in the next place, that the person who found the watch, should, after some time, discover that, in addition to all the properties which he had hitherto observed in it, it possessed the unexpected property of producing, in the course of its movement, another watch like itself (the thing is conceivable); that it contained within it a mechanism, a system of parts, a mould for instance, or a complex adjustment of lathes, files, and other tools, evidently and separately calculated for this purpose; let us inquire, what effect ought such a discovery to have upon his former conclusion.

I. The first effect would be to increase his admiration of the contrivance, and his conviction of the consummate skill of the contriver. Whether he regarded the object of the contrivance, the distinct apparatus, the intricate, yet in many parts intelligible mechanism, by which it was carried on, he would perceive, in this new observation, nothing but an additional reason for doing what he had already done,—for referring the construction of the watch to design, and to supreme art. If that construction without this property, or which is the same thing, before this property had been noticed, proved intention and art to have been employed about it; still more strong would the proof appear, when he came to the knowledge of this further property, the crown and perfection of all the rest.

II. He would reflect, that though the watch before him were, in some sense, the maker of the watch, which was fabricated in the course of its movements, yet it was in a very different sense from that, in which a carpenter, for instance, is the maker of a chair; the author of its contrivance, the cause of the relation of its parts to their use. With respect to these, the first watch was no cause at all to the second: in no such sense as this was it the author of the constitution and order, either of the parts which the new watch contained, or of the parts by the aid and instrumentality of which it was produced. We might possibly say, but with great latitude of expression, that a stream of water ground corn: but no latitude of expression would allow us to say, no stretch of conjecture could lead us to think, that the stream of water built the mill, though it were too ancient for us to know who the builder was. What the stream of water does in the affair, is neither more nor less than this; by the application of an unintelligent impulse to a mechanism previously arranged, arranged independently of it, and arranged by intelligence, an effect is produced, viz. the corn is ground. But the effect results from the arrangement. The force of the stream cannot be said to be the cause or author of the effect, still less of the arrangement. Understanding and plan in the formation of the mill were not the less necessary, for any share which the water has in grinding the corn: yet is this share the same, as that which the watch would have contributed to the production of the new watch, upon the supposition assumed in the last section. Therefore,

III. Though it be now no longer probable, that the individual watch, which our observer had found, was made immediately by the hand of an artificer, yet doth not this alteration in anywise affect the inference, that an artificer had been originally employed and concerned in the production. The argument from design remains as it was. Marks of design and contrivance are no more accounted for now, than they were before. In the same thing, we may ask for the cause of different properties. We may ask for the cause of the colour of a body, of its hardness, of its head; and these causes may be all different. We are now asking for the cause of that subserviency to a use, that relation to an end, which we have remarked in the watch before us. No answer is given to this question, by telling us that a preceding watch produced it. There cannot be design without a designer; contrivance without a contriver; order without choice; arrangement, without any thing capable of arranging; subserviency and relation to a purpose, without that which could intend a purpose; means suitable to an end, and executing their office, in accomplishing that end, without the end ever having been contemplated, or the means accommodated to it. Arrangement, disposition of parts, subserviency of means to an end, relation of instruments to a use, imply the presence of intelligence and mind. No one, therefore, can rationally believe, that the insensible, inanimate watch, from which the watch before us issued, was the proper cause of the mechanism we so much admire in it;—could be truly said to have constructed the instrument, disposed its parts, assigned their office, determined their order, action, and mutual dependency, combined their several motions into one result, and that also a result connected with the utilities of other beings. All these properties, therefore, are as much unaccounted for, as they were before.

IV. Nor is any thing gained by running the difficulty farther back, i. e. by supposing the watch before us to have been produced from another watch, that from a former, and so on indefinitely. Our going back ever so far, brings us no nearer to the least degree of satisfaction upon the subject. Contrivance is still unaccounted for. We still want a contriver. A designing mind is neither supplied by this supposition, nor dispensed with. If the difficulty were diminished the further we went back, by going back indefinitely we might exhaust it. And this is the only case to which this sort of reasoning applies. Where there is a tendency, or, as we increase the number of terms, a continual approach towards a limit, there, by supposing the number of terms to be what is called infinite, we may conceive the limit to be attained: but where there is no such tendency, or approach, nothing is effected by lengthening the series. There is no difference as to the point in question (whatever there may be as to many points), between one series and another; between a series which is finite, and a series which is infinite. A chain, composed of an infinite number of links, can no more support itself, than a chain composed of a finite number of links. And of this we are assured (though we never can have tried the experiment), because, by increasing the number of links, from ten for instance to a hundred, from a hundred to a thousand, &c. we make not the smallest approach, we observe not the smallest tendency, towards self-support. There is no difference in this respect (yet there may be a great difference in several respects) between a chain of a greater or less length, between one chain and another, between one that is finite and one that is infinite. This very much resembles the case before us. The machine which we are inspecting, demonstrates, by its construction, contrivance and design. Contrivance must have had a contriver; design, a designer; whether the machine immediately proceeded from another machine or not. That circumstance alters not the case. That other machine may, in like manner, have proceeded from a former machine: nor does that alter the case; contrivance must have had a contriver. That former one from one preceding it: no alteration still; a contriver is still necessary. No tendency is perceived, no approach towards a diminution of this necessity. It is the same with any and every succession of these machines; a succession of ten, of a hundred, of a thousand; with one series, as with another; a series which is finite, as with a series which is infinite. In whatever other respects they may differ, in this they do not. In all equally, contrivance and design are unaccounted for.

The question is not simply, How came the first watch into existence? which question, it may be pretended, is done away by supposing the series of watches thus produced from one another to have been infinite, and consequently to have had no-such first, for which it was necessary to provide a cause. This, perhaps, would have been nearly the state of the question, if no thing had been before us but an unorganized, unmechanized substance, without mark or indication of contrivance. It might be difficult to show that such substance could not have existed from eternity, either in succession (if it were possible, which I think it is not, for unorganized bodies to spring from one another), or by individual perpetuity. But that is not the question now. To suppose it to be so, is to suppose that it made no difference whether we had found a watch or a stone. As it is, the metaphysics of that question have no place; for, in the watch which we are examining, are seen contrivance, design; an end, a purpose; means for the end, adaptation to the purpose. And the question which irresistibly presses upon our thoughts, is, whence this contrivance and design? The thing required is the intending mind, the adapting hand, the intelligence by which that hand was directed. This question, this demand, is not shaken off, by increasing a number or succession of substances, destitute of these properties; nor the more, by increasing that number to infinity. If it be said, that, upon the supposition of one watch being produced from another in the course of that other's movements, and by means of the mechanism within it, we have a cause for the watch in my hand, viz. the watch from which it proceeded. I deny, that for the design, the contrivance, the suitableness of means to an end, the adaptation of instruments to a use (all which we discover in the watch), we have any cause whatever. It is in vain, therefore, to assign a series of such causes, or to allege that a series may be carried back to infinity; for I do not admit that we have yet any cause at all of the phænomena, still less any series of causes either finite or infinite. Here is contrivance, but no contriver; proofs of design, but no designer.

V. Our observer would further also reflect, that the maker of the watch before him, was, in truth and reality, the maker of every watch produced from it; there being no difference (except that the latter manifests a more exquisite skill) between the making of another watch with his own hands, by the mediation of files, lathes, chisels, &c. and the disposing, fixing, and inserting of these instruments, or of others equivalent to them, in the body of the watch already made in such a manner, as to form a new watch in the course of the movements which he had given to the old one. It is only working by one set of tools, instead of another.

The conclusion of which the first examination of the watch, of its works, construction, and movement, suggested, was, that it must have had, for the cause and author of that construction, an artificer, who understood its mechanism, and designed its use. This conclusion is invincible. A second examination presents us with a new discovery. The watch is found, in the course of its movement, to produce another watch, similar to itself; and not only so, but we perceive in it a system or organization, separately calculated for that purpose. What effect would this discovery have, or ought it to have, upon our former inference? What, as hath already been said, but to increase, beyond measure, our admiration of the skill, which had been employed in the formation of such a machine? Or shall it, instead of this, all at once turn us round to an opposite conclusion, viz. that no art or skill whatever has been concerned in the business, although all other evidences of art and skill remain as they were, and this last and supreme piece of art be now added to the rest? Can this be maintained without absurdity? Yet this is atheism.

Ludwig Feuerbach, *The Essence of Christianity*

God as a Projection of the Human Mind

In the perceptions of the senses consciousness of the object is distinguishable from consciousness of self; but in religion, consciousness of the object and self-consciousness coincide. The object of the senses is out of man, the religious object is within him, and therefore as little forsakes him as his self-consciousness or his conscience; it is the intimate, the closest object. "God", says Augustine, for example, "is nearer, more related to us, and therefore more easily known by us, than sensible, corporeal things." The object of the senses is in itself indifferent — independent of the disposition or of the judgment; but the object of religion is a selected object; the most excellent, the first, the supreme being; it essentially presupposes a critical judgment, a discrimination between the divine and the non-divine, between that which is worthy of adoration and that which is not worthy. And here may be applied, without any limitation, the proposition: the object of any subject is nothing else than the subject's own nature taken objectively. Such as are a man's thoughts and dispositions, such is his God; so much worth as a man has, so much and no more has his God. Consciousness of God is self-consciousness, knowledge of God is self-knowledge. By his God thou knowest the man, and by the man his God; the two are identical. Whatever is God to a man, that is his heart and soul; and conversely, God is the manifested inward nature, the expressed self of a man, — religion the solemn unveiling of a man's hidden treasures, the revelation of his intimate thoughts, the open confession of his love-secrets.

But when religion — consciousness of God — is designated as the self-consciousness of man, this is not to be understood as affirming that the religious man is directly aware of this identity; for, on the contrary, ignorance of it is fundamental to the peculiar nature of religion. To preclude this misconception, it is better to say, religion is man's earliest and also indirect form of self-knowledge. Hence, religion everywhere precedes philosophy, as in the history of the race, so also in that of the individual. Man first of all sees his nature as if out of himself, before he finds it in himself. His own nature is in the first instance contemplated by him as that of another being. Religion is the childlike condition of humanity; but the child sees his nature — man — out of himself; in childhood a man is an object to himself, under the form of another man. Hence the historical progress of religion consists in this: that what by an earlier religion was regarded as objective, is now recognized as subjective; that is, what was formerly contemplated and worshipped as God is now perceived to be something human. What was at first religion became at a later period idolatry; man is seen to have adored his own nature. Man has given objectivity to himself, but has not recognized the object as his own nature: a later religion takes this forward step; every advance in religion is therefore a deeper self-knowledge. But every particular religion, while it pronounces its predecessors idolatrous, excepts itself — and necessarily so, otherwise it would no longer be religion — from the fate, the common nature of all religions: it imputes only to other religions what is the fault, if fault it be, of religion in general. Because it has a different object, a different tenor, because it has transcended the ideas of preceding religions, it erroneously supposes itself exalted above the necessary eternal laws which constitute the essence of religion — it fancies its object, its ideas, to be superhuman. But the essence of religion, thus hidden from the religious, is evident to the thinker, by whom religion is viewed objectively, which it cannot be by its votaries. And it is our task to show that the antithesis of divine and human is altogether illusory, that is nothing else than the antithesis between the human nature in general and the human individual; that, consequently, the object and contents of the Christian religion are altogether human.

Religion, at least the Christian, is the relation of man to himself, or more correctly to his own nature (i.e., his subjective nature); but a relation to it, viewed as a nature apart from his own. The divine being is nothing else than the human being, or, rather, the human nature purified, freed from the limits of the individual man, made objective — i.e., contemplated and revered as another, a distinct being. All the attributes of the divine nature are, therefore, attributes of the human nature.

In relation to the attributes, the predicates, of the Divine Being, this is admitted without hesitation, but by no means in relation to the subject of these predicates. The negation of the subject is held to be irreligion, nay, atheism; though not so the negation of the predicates. But that which has no predicates or qualities, has no effect upon me; that which has no effect upon me has no existence for me. To deny all the qualities of a being is equivalent to denying the being himself. A being without qualities is one which cannot become an object to the mind, and such a being is virtually non-existent. Where man deprives God of all qualities, God is no longer anything more to him than a negative being. To the truly religious man, God is not a being without qualities, because to him he is a positive, real being. The theory that God cannot be defined, and consequently cannot be known by man, is therefore the offspring of recent times, a product of modern unbelief.

As reason is and can be pronounced finite only where man regards sensual enjoyment, or religious emotion, or aesthetic contemplation, or moral sentiment, as the absolute, the true; so the proposition that God is unknowable or undefinable, can only be enunciated and become fixed as a dogma, where this object has no longer any interest for the intellect; where the real, the positive, alone has any hold on man, where the real alone has for him the significance of the essential, of the absolute, divine object, but where at the same time, in contradiction with this purely worldly tendency, there yet exist some old remains of religiousness. On the ground that God is unknowable, man excuses himself to what is yet remaining of his religious conscience for his forgetfulness of God, his absorption in the world: he denies God practically by his conduct, — the world has possession of all his thoughts and inclinations, — but he does not deny him theoretically, he does not attack his existence; he lets that rest. But this existence does not affect or incommode him; it is a merely negative existence, an existence without existence, a self-contradictory existence, — a state of being which, as to its effects, is not distinguishable from non-being. The denial of determinate, positive predicates concerning the divine nature is nothing else than a denial of religion, with, however, an appearance of religion in its favor, so that it is not recognized as a denial; it is simply a subtle, disguised atheism. The alleged religious horror of limiting God by positive predicates is only the irreligious wish to know nothing more of God, to banish God from the mind. Dread of limitation is dread of existence. All real existence, i.e., all existence which is truly such, is qualitative, determinative existence. He who earnestly believes in the Divine existence is not shocked at the attributing even of gross sensuous qualities to God. He who dreads an existence that may give offense, who shrinks from the grossness of a positive predicate, may as well renounce existence altogether. A God who is injured by determinate qualities has not the courage and the strength to exist. Qualities are the fire, the vital breath, the oxygen, the salt of existence. An existence in general, an existence without qualities, is an insipidity, an absurdity. But there can be no more in God than is supplied by religion. Only where man loses his taste for religion, and thus religion itself becomes insipid, does the existence of God become an insipid existence — an existence without qualities.

There is, however, a still milder way of denying the divine predicates than the direct one just described. It is admitted that the predicates of the divine nature are finite, and, more particularly, human qualities, but their rejection is rejected; they are even taken under protection, because it is necessary to man to have a definite conception of God, and since he is man he can form no other than a human conception of him. In relation to God, it is said, these predicates are certainly without any objective validity; but to me, if he is to exist for me, he cannot appear otherwise than as he does appear to me, namely, as a being with attributes analogous to the human. But this distinction between what God is in himself, and what he is for me destroys the peace of religion, and is besides in itself an unfounded and untenable distinction. I cannot know whether God is something else in himself or for himself than he is for me; what he is to me is to me all that he is. For me, there lies in these predicates under which he exists for me, what he is in himself, his very nature; he is for me what he can alone ever be for me. The religious man finds perfect satisfaction in that which God is in relation to himself; of any other relation he knows nothing, for God is to him what he alone can be to man. In the distinction above stated, man takes a point of view above himself, i.e., above his nature, the absolute measure of his being; but this transcendentalism is only an illusion; for I can make the distinction between the object as it is in itself, and the object as it is for me, only where an object can really appear otherwise to me, not where it appears to me such as the absolute measure of my nature determines it to appear — such as it must appear to me. It is true that I may have a merely subjective conception, i.e., one which does not arise out of the general constitution of my species; but if my conception is determined by the constitution of my species, the distinction between what an object is in itself, and what is for me ceases; for this conception is itself an absolute one. The measure of the species is in the absolute measure, law, and criterion of man. And, indeed, religion has the conviction that its conceptions, its predicates of God, are such as every man ought to have, and must have, if he would have the true ones — that they are the conceptions necessary to human nature; nay, further, that they are objectively true, representing God as he is. To every religion the gods of other religions are only notions concerning God, but its own conception of God is to it God himself, the true God — God such as he is in himself. Religion is satisfied only with a complete Deity, a God without reservation; it will not have a mere phantasm of God; it demands God himself. Religion gives up its own existence when it gives up the nature of God; it is no longer a truth when it renounces the possession of the true God. Skepticism is the arch-enemy of religion; but the distinction between object and conception — between God as he is in himself, and God as he is for me — is a skeptical distinction, and therefore an irreligious one.

That which is to man the self-existent, the highest being, to which he can conceive nothing higher — that is to him the Divine Being. How then should he inquire concerning this being, what he is in himself? If God were an object to the bird, he would be a winged being: the bird knows nothing higher, nothing more blissful, than the winged condition. How ludicrous would it be if this bird pronounced: To me God appears as a bird, but what he is in himself I know not. To the bird the highest nature is the bird-nature; take from the conception of this, and you take from him the conception of the highest being. How, then, could he ask whether God in himself were winged? To ask whether God is in himself what he is for me, is to ask whether God is God, is to lift oneself above one's God, to rise up against him.

Wherever, therefore, this idea, that the religious predicates are only anthropomorphisms, has taken possession of a man, there has doubt, has unbelief, obtained the mastery of faith. And it is only the inconsequence of faint-heartedness and intellectual imbecility which does not proceed from this idea to the formal negation of the predicates, and from thence to the negation of the subject to which they relate. If thou doubtest the objective truth of the predicates, thou must also doubt the objective truth of the subject whose predicates they are. If thy predicates are anthropomorphisms, the subject of them is an anthropomorphism too. If love, goodness, personality, etc., are human attributes, so also is the subject which thou presupposest, the existence of God, the belief that there is a God, an anthropomorphism — a presupposition purely human.

Bertrand Russell, "Why I Am Not A Christian"

(March 6, 1927, South London branch Battersea Town Hall)

The Existence Of God

To come to this question of the existence of God: it is a large and serious question, and if I were to attempt to deal with it in any adequate manner I should have to keep you here until Kingdom Come, so that you will have to excuse me if I deal with it in a somewhat summary fashion. You know, of course, that the Catholic Church has laid it down as dogma that the existence of God can be proved by the unaided reason. This is a somewhat curious dogma, but it is one of their dogmas. They had to introduce it because at one time the freethinkers adopted the habit of saying that there were such and such arguments which mere reason might urge against the existence of God, but of course they knew as a matter of faith that God did exist. The arguments and reasons were set out at great length, and the Catholic Church felt that they must stop it. Therefore they laid it down as dogma that the existence of God can be proved by the unaided reason and they had to set up what they considered were arguments to prove it.

The First Cause Argument

Perhaps the simplest and easiest to understand is the argument of the First Cause. (It is maintained that everything we see in the world has a cause, and as you go back in the chain of causes further and further you must come to a First Cause, and to that First Cause you give the name of God.) That argument, I suppose, does not carry much weight nowadays, because, in the first place, cause is not quite what it used to be. The philosophers and the men of science have got going on cause, and it has not anything like the vitality it used to have; but apart from that, you can see that the argument that there must be a First Cause is one that cannot have any validity. I may say that when I was a young man and was debating these questions very seriously in my mind, I for a long time accepted the argument of the First Cause, until one day, at the age of eighteen, I read John Stuart Mill's autobiography, and I there found this sentence: "My father taught me that the question 'Who made me?' cannot be answered, since it immediately suggests the further question "Who made god'" that very simple sentence showed me, as I still think, the fallacy in the argument of the First Cause. If everything must have a cause, then God must have a cause. If there can be anything without a cause, it may just as well be the world as God, so that there cannot be any validity in that argument. It is exactly of the same nature as the Hindu's view, that the world rested upon an elephant, and the elephant rested upon a tortoise; and when they said, "How about the tortoise?" the Indian said, "Suppose we change the subject." The argument is really no better than that. There is no reason why the world could not have come into being without a cause; nor, on the other hand, is there any reason why it should not have always existed. There is no reason to suppose that the world had a beginning at all. The idea that things must have a beginning is really due to the poverty of our imagination. Therefore, perhaps, I need not waste any more time upon the argument about the First Cause.

The Natural-Law Argument

Then there is a very common argument from Natural Law. That was a favorite argument all through the eighteenth century, especially under the influence of Sir Isaac Newton and his cosmogony. People observed the planets going around the sun according to the law of gravitation, and the thought that God had given a behest to these planets to move in a particular fashion, and that was why they did so. That was, of course, a convenient and simple explanation that saved them the trouble of looking any further for any explanation of the law of gravitation. Nowadays we explain the law of gravitation in a somewhat complicated fashion that Einstein has introduced. I do not propose to give you a lecture on the law of gravitation, as interpreted by Einstein, because that again would take some time; at any rate, you no longer have the sort of Natural Law that you had in the Newtonian system, where, for some reason that nobody could understand, nature behaved in a uniform fashion.

We now find that a great many things we thought were Natural Laws are really human conventions. You know that even in the remotest depth of stellar space there are still three feet to a yard. That is, no doubt, a very remarkable fact, but you would hardly call it a law of nature. And a great many things that have been regarded as laws of nature are of that kind. On the other hand, where you can get down to any knowledge of what atoms actually do, you will find they are much less subject to law than people thought, and the laws at which you arrive are statistical averages of just the sort that would emerge from chance. There is, as we all know, a law that says if you throw dice you will get double sixes only about once in thirty-six times, and we do not regard that as evidence to the contrary that the fall of the dice is regulated by design; on the contrary, if the double sixes came every time we should think that there was design. The laws of nature are of that sort as regards to a great many of them. They are statistical averages such as would emerge from the laws of chance; and that makes the whole business of natural law much less impressive than it formerly was. Quite apart from that, which represents the momentary state of science that may change tomorrow, the whole idea that natural laws imply a lawgiver is due to a confusion between natural and human laws. Human laws are behests commanding you to behave a certain way, in which you may choose to behave, or you may choose not to behave; but natural laws are a description of how things do in fact behave, and being a mere description of what they in fact do, you cannot argue that there must be supposedly someone who told them to do that, because even supposing there were, you are faced with the question, "Why did god issue just those and no others?" If you say that he did it simply from his own good pleasure, and without any reason, you then find that there is something which is not subject to law, and so your train of natural law is interrupted. If you say, as more orthodox theologians do, that in all the laws which God issues he had a reason for giving those laws rather than others — the reason, of course, being to create the best universe, although you would never think it to look at it — if there were a reason for the laws which God gave, then God himself was subject to law, and therefore you do not get any advantage by introducing God as an intermediary. You really have a law outside and anterior to the divine edicts, and God does not serve your purpose, as he is not the ultimate lawgiver. In short, this whole argument from natural law no longer has anything like the strength that it used to have. I am traveling on in time in my review of these arguments. The arguments that are used for the existence of God change their character as time goes on. They were at first hard intellectual arguments embodying certain quite definite fallacies. As we come to modern times they become less respectable intellectually and more and more affected by a kind of moralizing vagueness.

The Argument from Design

The next step in the process brings us to the argument from design. You all know the argument from design: everything in the world is made just so that we can manage to live in the world, and if the world was ever so little different, we could not manage to live in it. That is the argument from design. It sometimes takes a rather curious form; for instance, it is argued that rabbits have white tails in order to be easy to shoot. I do not know how rabbits would view that application. It is an easy argument to parody. You all know Voltaire's remark, that obviously the nose was designed to be such as to fit spectacles. That sort of parody has turned out to be not nearly so wide of the mark as it might have seemed in the eighteenth century, because since the time of Darwin we understand much better why living creatures are adapted to their environment. It is not that their environment was made to be suitable to them, but that they grew to be suitable to it, that is the basis of adaptation. There is no evidence of design about it.

When you come to look into this argument from design, it is a most astonishing thing that people can believe that this world, with all the things that are in it, with all its defects, should be the best that omnipotence and omniscience have been able to produce in millions of years. I really cannot believe it. Do you think that, if you were granted omnipotence and omniscience and millions of years in which to perfect your world, you could produce nothing better than the Ku Klux Klan or the fascists? Moreover, if you accept the ordinary laws of science, you have to suppose that human life and life in general on this planet will die out in due course: it is a stage in the decay of the solar system; at a certain stage of decay you get the sort of conditions and temperature and so forth which are suitable to protoplasm, and there is life for a short time in the life of the whole solar system. You see in the moon the sort of thing to which the earth is tending — something dead, cold, and lifeless.

I am told that that sort of view is depressing, and people will sometimes tell you that if they believed that, they would not be able to go on living. Do not believe it; it is all nonsense. Nobody really worries about what is going to happen millions of years hence. Even if they think they are worrying much about that, they are really deceiving themselves. They are worried about something much more mundane, or it may merely be bad digestion; but nobody is really seriously rendered unhappy by the thought of something that is going to happen in this world millions and millions of years hence. Therefore, although it is of course a gloomy view to suppose that life will die out — at least I suppose we may say so, although sometimes when I contemplate the things that people do with their lives I think it is almost a consolation — it is not such as to render life miserable. It merely makes you turn your attention to other things.

The Moral Arguments for Deity

Now we reach one stage further in what I shall call the intellectual descent that the Theists have made in their argumentations, and we come to what are called moral arguments for the existence of God. You all know, of course, that there used to be in the old days three intellectual arguments for the existence of God, all of which were disposed of by Immanuel Kant in the "Critique of Pure Reason;" but no sooner had he disposed of those arguments than he invented a new one, a moral argument, and that quite convinced him. He was like many people: in intellectual matters he was skeptical, but in moral matters he believed implicitly in the maxims that he had imbibed at his mother's knee. That illustrates what the psychoanalysts so much emphasize — the immensely stronger hold that our very early associations have than those of later times.

Kant, as I say, invented a new moral argument for the existence of God, and that in varying forms was extremely popular during the nineteenth century. it has all sorts of forms. One form is to say there would be no right and wrong unless god existed. I am not for the moment concerned with whether there is a difference between right and wrong, or whether there is not: that is another question. The point I am concerned with is that, if you are quite sure there is a difference between right and wrong, then you are in this situation: is that difference due to God's fiat or is it not? If it is due to God's fiat, then for God himself there is no difference between right and wrong, and it is no longer a significant statement to say that God is good. If you are going to say, as theologians do, that God is good, you must then say that right and wrong have some meaning which is independent of God's fiat, because God's fiats are good and not bad independently of the fact that he made them. If you are going to say that, you will have to say that it is not only through God that right and wrong came into being, but that they are in their essence logically anterior to God. you could, of course, if you liked, say that there was a superior deity who gave orders to the God that made this world, or could take up a line that some of the Gnostics took up — a line which I often thought was a very plausible one — that as a matter of fact this world that we know was made by the Devil at a moment when God was not looking. There is a good deal to be said for that, and I am not concerned to refute it.

The Argument for the Remedying of Injustice

Then there is another very curious form of moral argument, which is this: they say that the existence of God is required to bring justice into the world. In the part of the universe that we know there is a great injustice, and often the good suffer, and the often the wicked prosper, and one hardly knows which of those is more annoying; but if you are going to have justice in the universe as a whole you have to suppose a future life to redress the balance of life here on earth. So they say that there must be a God, and that there must be Heaven and Hell in order that in the long run there may be justice. That is a very curious argument. If you looked at the matter from a scientific point of view, you would say, "After all, I only know this world. I do not know about the rest of the universe, but so far as one can argue from probabilities one would say that probably this world is a fair sample, and if there is injustice here then the odds are great that there is injustice elsewhere also." Supposing you got a crate of oranges that you opened, and you found all the top layer of oranges bad, you would not argue, "The underneath ones must be good, so as to redress the balance." You would say, "Probably the whole lot is a bad consignment"; and that is really what a scientific person would argue about the universe. He would say, "Here we find in this world a great deal of injustice, and so far as that goes that is a reason for supposing that justice does not rule in this world, and therefore so far as it goes it supports a moral argument against deity and not in favor of one." Of course I know that the sort of intellectual arguments that I have been talking to you about is not really what moves people. What really moves people to believe in God is not any intellectual argument at all. Most people believe in God because they have been taught from early infancy to do it, and that is the main reason.

Then I think that the next most powerful reason is the wish for safety, a sort of feeling that there is a big brother who will look after you. That plays a very profound part in influencing people's desire for a belief in God.

Michael J. Behe: *Molecular Machines: Experimental Support for the Design Inference*

A Series of Eyes

How do we see? In the 19th century the anatomy of the eye was known in great detail and the sophisticated mechanisms it employs to deliver an accurate picture of the outside world astounded everyone who was familiar with them. Scientists of the 19th century correctly observed that if a person were so unfortunate as to be missing one of the eye's many integrated features, such as the lens, or iris, or ocular muscles, the inevitable result would be a severe loss of vision or outright blindness. Thus it was concluded that the eye could only function if it were nearly intact.

As Charles Darwin was considering possible objections to his theory of evolution by natural selection in The Origin of Species he discussed the problem of the eye in a section of the book appropriately entitled "Organs of Extreme Perfection and Complication." He realized that if in one generation an organ of the complexity of the eye suddenly appeared, the event would be tantamount to a miracle. Somehow, for Darwinian evolution to be believable, the difficulty that the public had in envisioning the gradual formation of complex organs had to be removed.

Darwin succeeded brilliantly, not by actually describing a real pathway that evolution might have used in constructing the eye, but rather by pointing to a variety of animals that were known to have eyes of various constructions, ranging from a simple light sensitive spot to the complex vertebrate camera eye, and suggesting that the evolution of the human eye might have involved similar organs as intermediates.

But the question remains, how do we see? Although Darwin was able to persuade much of the world that a modern eye could be produced gradually from a much simpler structure, he did not even attempt to explain how the simple light sensitive spot that was his starting point actually worked. When discussing the eye Darwin dismissed the question of its ultimate mechanism[1]:

How a nerve comes to be sensitive to light hardly concerns us more than how life itself originated.

He had an excellent reason for declining to answer the question: 19th century science had not progressed to the point where the matter could even be approached. The question of how the eye works--that is, what happens when a photon of light first impinges on the retina--simply could not be answered at that time. As a matter of fact, no question about the underlying mechanism of life could be answered at that time. How do animal muscles cause movement? How does photosynthesis work? How is energy extracted from food? How does the body fight infection? Nobody knew.

Calvinism

Now, it appears to be a characteristic of the human mind that when it is unconstrained by knowledge of the mechanisms of a process, then it seems easy to imagine simple steps leading from non-function to function. A happy example of this is seen in the popular comic strip Calvin and Hobbes. Little boy Calvin is always having adventures in the company of his tiger Hobbes by jumping in a box and traveling back in time, or grabbing a toy ray gun and "transmogrifying" himself into various animal shapes, or again using a box as a duplicator and making copies of himself to deal with worldly powers such as his mom and his teachers. A small child such as Calvin finds it easy to imagine that a box just might be able to fly like an airplane (or something), because Calvin does not know how airplanes work.

A good example from the biological world of complex changes appearing to be simple is the belief in spontaneous generation. One of the chief proponents of the theory of spontaneous generation during the middle of the 19th century was Ernst Haeckel, a great admirer of Darwin and an eager popularizer of Darwin's theory. From the limited view of cells that 19th century microscopes provided, Haeckel believed that a cell was a "simple little lump of albuminous combination of carbon," [2] not much different from a piece of microscopic Jello. Thus it seemed to Haeckel that such simple life could easily be produced from inanimate material. In 1859, the year of the publication of The Origin of Species, an exploratory vessel, H.M.S. Cyclops, dredged up some curious looking mud from the sea bottom. Eventually Haeckel came to observe the mud and thought that it closely resembled some cells he had seen under a microscope. Excitedly he brought this to the attention of Thomas Henry Huxley, Darwin's great friend and defender. Huxley, too, became convinced that it was Urschleim (that is, protoplasm), the progenitor of life itself, and Huxley named the mud Bathybius Haeckelii after the eminent proponent of abiogenesis.

The mud failed to grow. In later years, with the development of new biochemical techniques and improved microscopes, the complexity of the cell was revealed. The "simple lumps" were shown to contain thousands of different types of organic molecules, proteins, and nucleic acids, many discrete subcellular structures, specialized compartments for specialized processes, and an extremely complicated architecture. Looking back from the perspective of our time, the episode of Bathybius Haeckelii seems silly or downright embarrassing, but it shouldn't. Haeckel and Huxley were behaving naturally, like Calvin: since they were unaware of the complexity of cells, they found it easy to believe that cells could originate from simple mud.

Throughout history there have been many other examples, similar to that of Haeckel, Huxley and the cell, where a key piece of a particular scientific puzzle was beyond the understanding of the age. In science there is even a whimsical term for a machine or structure or process that does something, but the actual mechanism by which it accomplishes its task is unknown: it is called a 'black box.' In Darwin's time all of biology was a black box: not only the cell, or the eye, or digestion, or immunity, but every biological structure and function because, ultimately, no one could explain how biological processes occurred.

Ernst Mayr, the prominent biologist, historian, and guiding force behind the neo-Darwinian synthesis, has pointed out that [3]:

Any scientific revolution has to accept all sorts of black boxes, for if one had to wait until all black boxes are opened, one would never have any conceptual advances.

That is true. But in earlier days when black boxes were finally opened science, and sometimes the whole world, appeared to change. Biology has progressed tremendously due to the model that Darwin put forth. But the black boxes Darwin accepted are now being opened, and our view of the world is again being shaken.

Proteins

In order to understand the molecular basis of life it is necessary to understand how things called "proteins" work. Although most people think of protein" as something you eat, one of the major food groups, when they reside in the body of an uneaten animal or plant proteins serve a different purpose. Proteins are the machinery of living tissue that builds the structures and carries out the chemical reactions necessary for life. For example, the first of many steps necessary for the conversion of sugar to biologically-usable forms of energy is carried out by a protein called hexokinase. Skin is made in large measure of a protein called collagen. When light impinges on your retina it interacts first with a protein called rhodopsin. As can be seen even by this limited number of examples proteins carry out amazingly diverse functions. However, in general a given protein can perform only one or a few functions: rhodopsin cannot form skin and collagen cannot interact usefully with light. Therefore a typical cell contains thousands and thousands of different types of proteins to perform the many tasks necessary for life, much like a carpenter's workshop might contain many different kinds of tools for various carpentry work.

What do these versatile tools look like? The basic structure of proteins is quite simple: they are formed by hooking together in a chain discrete subunits called amino acids. Although the protein chain can consist of anywhere from about 50 to about 1,000 amino acid links, each position can only contain one of twenty different amino acids. In this way they are much like words: words can come in various lengths but they are made up from a discrete set of 26 letters. Now, a protein in a cell does not float around like a floppy chain; rather, it folds up into a very precise structure which can be quite different for different types of proteins. When all is said and done two different amino sequences--two different proteins--can be folded to structures as specific as and different from each other as a three-eighths inch wrench and a jigsaw. And like the household tools, if the shape of the proteins is significantly warped then they fail to do their jobs.

The Eyesight of Man

In general, biological processes on the molecular level are performed by networks of proteins, each member of which carries out a particular task in a chain.

Let us return to the question, how do we see? Although to Darwin the primary event of vision was a black box, through the efforts of many biochemists an answer to the question of sight is at hand. [4] When light strikes the retina a photon is absorbed by an organic molecule called 11-cis-retinal, causing it to rearrange within picoseconds to trans-retinal. The change in shape of retinal forces a corresponding change in shape of the protein, rhodopsin, to which it is tightly bound. As a consequence of the protein's metamorphosis, the behavior of the protein changes in a very specific way. The altered protein can now interact with another protein called transducin. Before associating with rhodopsin, transducin is tightly bound to a small organic molecule called GDP, but when it binds to rhodopsin the GDP dissociates itself from transducin and a molecule called GTP, which is closely related to, but critically different from, GDP, binds to transducin.

The exchange of GTP for GDP in the transducinrhodopsin complex alters its behavior. GTP-transducinrhodopsin binds to a protein called phosphodiesterase, located in the inner membrane of the cell. When bound by rhodopsin and its entourage, the phosphodiesterase acquires the ability to chemically cleave a molecule called cGMP. Initially there are a lot of cGMP molecules in the cell, but the action of the phosphodiesterase lowers the concentration of cGMP. Activating the phosphodiesterase can be likened to pulling the plug in a bathtub, lowering the level of water.

A second membrane protein which binds cGMP, called an ion channel, can be thought of as a special gateway regulating the number of sodium ions in the cell. The ion channel normally allows sodium ions to flow into the cell, while a separate protein actively pumps them out again. The dual action of the ion channel and pump proteins keeps the level of sodium ions in the cell within a narrow range. When the concentration of cGMP is reduced from its normal value through cleavage by the phosphodiesterase, many channels close, resulting in a reduced cellular concentration of positively charged sodium ions. This causes an imbalance of charges across the cell membrane which, finally, causes a current to be transmitted down the optic nerve to the brain: the result, when interpreted by the brain, is vision.

If the biochemistry of vision were limited to the reactions listed above, the cell would quickly deplete its supply of 11-cis-retinal and cGMP while also becoming depleted of sodium ions. Thus a system is required to limit the signal that is generated and restore the cell to its original state; there are several mechanisms which do this. Normally, in the dark, the ion channel, in addition to sodium ions, also allows calcium ions to enter the cell; calcium is pumped back out by a different protein in order to maintain a constant intracellular calcium concentration. However, when cGMP levels fall, shutting down the ion channel and decreasing the sodium ion concentration, calcium ion concentration is also decreased. The phosphodiesterase enzyme, which destroys cGMP, is greatly slowed down at lower calcium concentration. Additionally, a protein called guanylate cyclase begins to resynthesize cGMP when calcium levels start to fall. Meanwhile, while all of this is going on, metarhodopsin II is chemically modified by an enzyme called rhodopsin kinase, which places a phosphate group on its substrate. The modified rhodopsin is then bound by a protein dubbed arrestin, which prevents the rhodopsin from further activating transducin. Thus the cell contains mechanisms to limit the amplified signal started by a single photon.

Trans-retinal eventually falls off of the rhodopsin molecule and must be reconverted to 11-cis-retinal and again bound by opsin to regenerate rhodopsin for another visual cycle. To accomplish this trans-retinal is first chemically modified by an enzyme to transretinol, a form containing two more hydrogen atoms. A second enzyme then isomerizes the molecule to 11-cis-retinol. Finally, a third enzyme removes the previouslyadded hydrogen atoms to form 11-cis-retinal, and the cycle is complete.

To Explain Life

Although many details of the biochemistry of vision have not been cited here, the overview just seen is meant to demonstrate that, ultimately, this is what it means to 'explain' vision. This is the level of explanation that Biological science eventually must aim for. In order to say that some function is understood, every relevant step in the process must be elucidated. The relevant steps in biological processes occur ultimately at the molecular level, so a satisfactory explanation of a biological phenomenon such as sight, or digestion, or immunity, must include a molecular explanation. It is no longer sufficient, now that the black box of vision has been opened, for an 'evolutionary explanation' of that power to invoke only the anatomical structures of whole eyes, as Darwin did in the 19th century and as most popularizers of evolution continue to do today. Anatomy is, quite simply, irrelevant. So is the fossil record. It does not matter whether or not the fossil record is consistent with evolutionary theory, any more than it mattered in physics that Newton's theory was consistent with everyday experience. The fossil record has nothing to tell us about, say, whether or how the interactions of 11-cis-retinal with rhodopsin, transducin, and phosphodiesterase could have developed step-by-step. Neither do the patterns of biogeography matter, or of population genetics, or the explanations that evolutionary theory has given for rudimentary organs or species abundance.

"How a nerve comes to be sensitive to light hardly concerns us more than how life itself originated," said Darwin in the 19th century. But both phenomena have attracted the interest of modern biochemistry. The story of the slow paralysis of research on life's origin is quite interesting, but space precludes its retelling here. Suffice it to say that at present the field of originoflife studies has dissolved into a cacophony of conflicting models, each unconvincing, seriously incomplete, and incompatible with competing models. In private even most evolutionary biologists will admit that science has no explanation for the beginning of life. [5]

The purpose of this paper is to show that the same problems which beset origin-of-life research also bedevil efforts to show how virtually any complex biochemical system came about. Biochemistry has revealed a molecular world which stoutly resists explanation by the same theory that has long been applied at the level of the whole organism. Neither of Darwin's black boxes--the origin of life or the origin of vision or other complex biochemical systems--has been accounted for by his theory.

Irreducible Complexity

In *The Origin of Species* Darwin stated [6]:

> If it could be demonstrated that any complex organ existed which could not possibly have been formed by numerous, successive, slight modifications, my theory would absolutely break down.

A system which meets Darwin's criterion is one which exhibits irreducible complexity. By irreducible complexity I mean a single system which is composed of several interacting parts that contribute to the basic function, and where the removal of any one of the parts causes the system to effectively cease functioning. An irreducibly complex system cannot be produced gradually by slight, successive modifications of a precursor system, since any precursor to an irreducibly complex system is by definition nonfunctional. Since natural selection requires a function to select, an irreducibly complex biological system, if there is such a thing, would have to arise as an integrated unit for natural selection to have anything to act on. It is almost universally conceded that such a sudden event would be irreconcilable with the gradualism Darwin envisioned. At this point, however, 'irreducibly complex' is just a term, whose power resides mostly in its definition. We must now ask if any real thing is in fact irreducibly complex, and, if so, then are any irreducibly complex things also biological systems.

Consider the humble mousetrap (Figure 1). The mousetraps that my family uses in our home to deal with unwelcome rodents consist of a number of parts. There are: (1) a flat wooden platform to act as a base; (2) a metal hammer, which does the actual job of crushing the little mouse; (3) a wire spring with extended ends to press against the platform and the hammer when the trap is charged; (4) a sensitive catch which releases when slight pressure is applied; and (5) a metal bar which holds the hammer back when the trap is charged and connects to the catch. There are also assorted staples and screws to hold the system together.

Figure 1. A household mousetrap. The working parts of the trap are labeled. If any of the parts are missing the trap does not function.

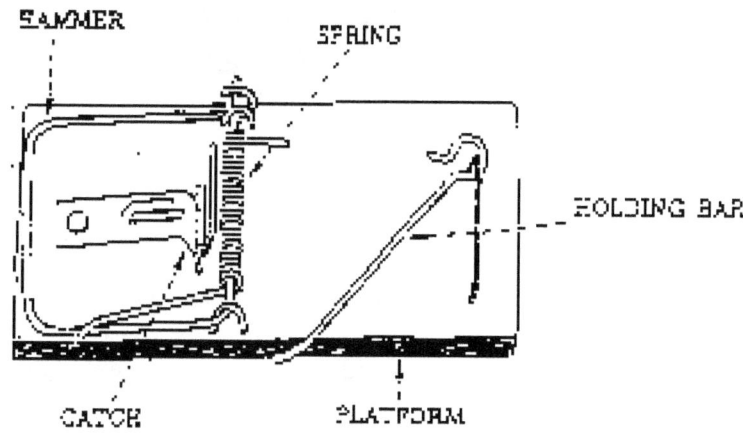

If any one of the components of the mousetrap (the base, hammer, spring, catch, or holding bar) is removed, then the trap does not function. In other words, the simple little mousetrap has no ability to trap a mouse until several separate parts are all assembled.

Because the mousetrap is necessarily composed of several parts, it is irreducibly complex. Thus, irreducibly complex systems exist.

Molecular Machines

Now, are any biochemical systems irreducibly complex? Yes, it turns out that many are.

Earlier we discussed proteins. In many biological structures proteins are simply components of larger molecular machines. Like the picture tube, wires, metal bolts and screws that comprise a television set, many proteins are part of structures that only function when virtually all of the components have been assembled. A good example of this is a cilium. [7]

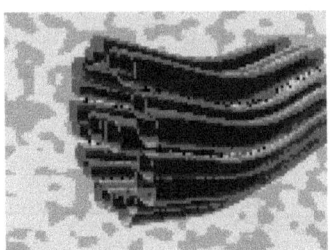

Figure 2a. Animation of a Cilium

Cilia are hairlike organelles on the surfaces of many animal and lower plant cells that serve to move fluid over the cell's surface or to "row" single cells through a fluid. In humans, for example, epithelial cells lining the respiratory tract each have about 200 cilia that beat in synchrony to sweep mucus towards the throat for elimination. A cilium consists of a membrane-coated bundle of fibers called an axoneme. An axoneme contains a ring of 9 double microtubules surrounding two central single microtubules. Each outer doublet consists of a ring of 13 filaments (subfiber A) fused to an assembly of 10 filaments (subfiber B). The filaments of the microtubules are composed of two proteins called alpha and beta tubulin. The 11 microtubules forming an axoneme are held together by three types of connectors: subfibers A are joined to the central microtubules by radial spokes; adjacent outer doublets are joined by linkers that consist of a highly elastic protein called nexin; and the central microtubules are joined by a connecting bridge. Finally, every subfiber A bears two arms, an inner arm and an outer arm, both containing the protein dynein.

But how does a cilium work? Experiments have indicated that ciliary motion results from the chemically-powered "walking" of the dynein arms on one microtubule up the neighboring subfiber B of a second microtubule so that the two microtubules slide past each other (Figure 2a and b). However, the protein cross-links between microtubules in an intact cilium prevent neighboring microtubules from sliding past each other by more than a short distance. These cross-links, therefore, convert the dynein-induced sliding motion to a bending motion of the entire axoneme.

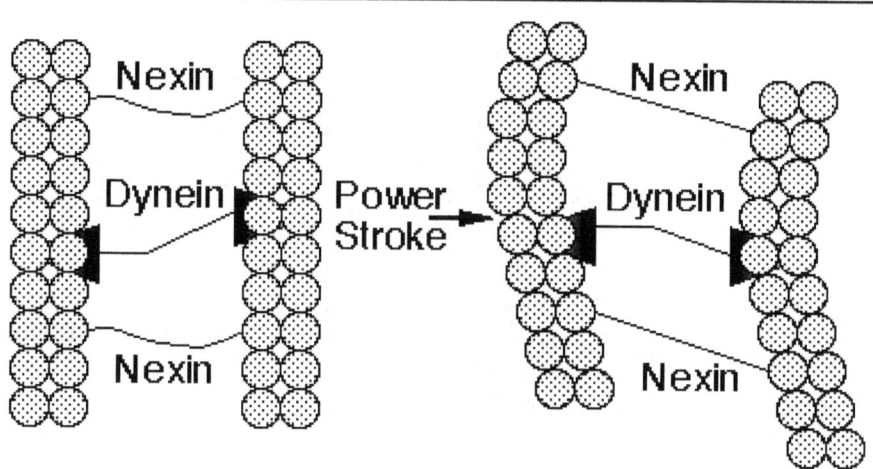

Figure 2b. Schematic drawing of part of a cilium. The power stroke of the motor protein, dynein, attached to one microtubule, against subfiber B of a neighboring microtubule causes the fibers to slide past each other. The flexible linker protein, nexin, converts the sliding motion to a bending motion.

Now, let us sit back, review the workings of the cilium, and consider what it implies. Cilia are composed of at least a half dozen proteins: alpha-tubulin, beta-tubulin, dynein, nexin, spoke protein, and a central bridge protein. These combine to perform one task, ciliary motion, and all of these proteins must be present for the cilium to function. If the tubulins are absent, then there are no filaments to slide; if the dynein is missing, then the cilium remains rigid and motionless; if nexin or the other connecting proteins are missing, then the axoneme falls apart when the filaments slide.

What we see in the cilium, then, is not just profound complexity, but also irreducible complexity on the molecular scale. Recall that by "irreducible complexity" we mean an apparatus that requires several distinct components for the whole to work. My mousetrap must have a base, hammer, spring, catch, and holding bar, all working together, in order to function. Similarly, the cilium, as it is constituted, must have the sliding filaments, connecting proteins, and motor proteins for function to occur. In the absence of any one of those components, the apparatus is useless.

The components of cilia are single molecules. This means that there are no more black boxes to invoke; the complexity of the cilium is final, fundamental. And just as scientists, when they began to learn the complexities of the cell, realized how silly it was to think that life arose spontaneously in a single step or a few steps from ocean mud, so too we now realize that the complex cilium can not be reached in a single step or a few steps. But since the complexity of the cilium is irreducible, then it can not have functional precursors. Since the irreducibly complex cilium can not have functional precursors it can not be produced by natural selection, which requires a continuum of function to work. Natural selection is powerless when there is no function to select. We can go further and say that, if the cilium can not be produced by natural selection, then the cilium was designed.

The Study of "Molecular Evolution"

Other examples of irreducible complexity abound, including aspects of protein transport, blood clotting, closed circular DNA, electron transport, the bacterial flagellum, telomeres, photosynthesis, transcription regulation, and much more. Examples of irreducible complexity can be found on virtually every page of a biochemistry textbook. But if these things cannot be explained by Darwinian evolution, how has the scientific community regarded these phenomena of the past forty years? A good place to look for an answer to that question is in the Journal of Molecular Evolution. JME is a journal that was begun specifically to deal with the topic of how evolution occurs on the molecular level. It has high scientific standards, and is edited by prominent figures in the field. In a recent issue of JME there were published eleven articles; of these, all eleven were concerned simply with the analysis of protein or DNA sequences. None of the papers discussed detailed models for intermediates in the development of complex biomolecular structures. In the past ten years JME has published 886 papers. Of these, 95 discussed the chemical synthesis of molecules thought to be necessary for the origin of life, 44 proposed mathematical models to improve sequence analysis, 20 concerned the evolutionary implications of current structures, and 719 were analyses of protein or polynucleotide sequences. There were zero papers discussing detailed models for intermediates in the development of complex biomolecular structures. This is not a peculiarity of JME. No papers are to be found that discuss detailed models for intermediates in the development of complex biomolecular structures in the Proceedings of the National Academy of Science, Nature, Science, the Journal of Molecular Biology or, to my knowledge, any journal whatsoever.

Sequence comparisons overwhelmingly dominate the literature of molecular evolution. But sequence comparisons simply can't account for the development of complex biochemical systems any more than Darwin's comparison of simple and complex eyes told him how vision worked. Thus in this area science is mute. This means that when we infer that complex biochemical systems were designed, we are contradicting no experimental result, we are in conflict with no theoretical study. No experiments needs to be questioned, but the interpretation of all experiments must now be reexamined, just as the results of experiments that were consistent with a Newtonian view of the universe had to be reinterpreted when the waveparticle duality of matter was discerned.

Conclusion

It is often said that science must avoid any conclusions which smack of the supernatural. But this seems to me to be both bad logic and bad science. Science is not a game in which arbitrary rules are used to decide what explanations are to be permitted. Rather, it is an effort to make true statements about physical reality. It was only about sixty years ago that the expansion of the universe was first observed. This fact immediately suggested a singular event--that at some time in the distant past the universe began expanding from an extremely small size. To many people this inference was loaded with overtones of a supernatural event--the creation, the beginning of the universe. The prominent physicist A.S. Eddington probably spoke for many physicists in voicing his disgust with such a notion [8]:

Philosophically, the notion of an abrupt beginning to the present order of Nature is repugnant to me, as I think it must be to most;

and even those who would welcome a proof of the intervention of a Creator will probably consider that a single windingup at some remote epoch is not really the kind of relation between God and his world that brings satisfaction to the mind.

Nonetheless, the Big Bang hypothesis was embraced by physics and over the years has proven to be a very fruitful paradigm. The point here is that physics followed the data where it seemed to lead, even though some thought the model gave aid and comfort to religion. In the present day, as biochemistry multiplies examples of fantastically complex molecular systems, systems which discourage even an attempt to explain how they may have arisen, we should take a lesson from physics. The conclusion of design flows naturally from the data; we should not shrink from it; we should embrace it and build on it.

In concluding, it is important to realize that we are not inferring design from what we do not know, but from what we do know. We are not inferring design to account for a black box, but to account for an open box. A man from a primitive culture who sees an automobile might guess that it was powered by the wind or by an antelope hidden under the car, but when he opens up the hood and sees the engine he immediately realizes that it was designed. In the same way biochemistry has opened up the cell to examine what makes it run and we see that it, too, was designed.

It was a shock to people of the nineteenth century when they discovered, from observations science had made, that many features of the biological world could be ascribed to the elegant principle of natural selection. It is a shock to us in the twentieth century to discover, from observations science has made, that the fundamental mechanisms of life cannot be ascribed to natural selection, and therefore were designed. But we must deal with our shock as best we can and go on. The theory of undirected evolution is already dead, but the work of science continues.

This paper was originally presented in the Summer of 1994 at the meeting ofthe C.S. Lewis Society, Cambridge University.

References

1. Darwin, Charles (1872) Origin of Species 6th ed (1988), p.151, New York University Press, New York.
2. Farley, John (1979) The Spontaneous Generation Controversy from Descartes to Oparin, 2nd ed, p.73, The Johns Hopkins University Press, Baltimore.
3. Mayr, Ernst (1991) One Long Argument, p. 146, Harvard University Press, Cambridge.
4. Devlin, Thomas M. (1992) Textbook of Biochemistry, pp.938954, WileyLiss, New York.
5. University of Washington rhetorician John Angus Campbell has observed that "huge edifices of ideas such as positivism never really die. Thinking people gradually abandon them and even ridicule them among themselves, but keep the persuasively useful parts to scare away the uninformed." "The Comic Frame and the Rhetoric of Science: Epistemology and Ethics in Darwin's Origin," Rhetoric Society Quarterly 24, pp.2750 (1994). This certainly applies to the way the scientific community handles questions on the origin of life.
6. Darwin, p.154.
7. Voet, D. & Voet, J.G. (1990) Biochemistry, pp.11321139, John Wiley & Sons, New York.
8. Cited in Jaki, Stanley L. (1980) Cosmos and Creator, pp.56, Gateway Editions, Chicago.

Mike Behe received a Bachelor of Science degree in Chemistry from Drexel University in 1974 and the Ph.D. in Biochemistry from the University of Pennsylvania in 1978. After doing postdoctoral work at the National institutes of Health he became assistant professor of Chemistry at the City University of New York/Queens College.

In 1985 he moved to Lehigh University in Bethlehem, PA, where he is currently Associate Professor in the Department of Biological Sciences.

Mike is married to the former Celeste LaTassa. They are members of St. Theresa Parish in Hellertown, PA, where they are raising their six children: Grace, age 10; Benedict, 9; Clare, 7; Leo, 5; Rose, 3; and Vincent, 1.

Look for Dr. Behe's new book published by the Free Press, Darwin's Black Box: The Biochemical Challenge to Evolution.

Copyright © 1997 Michael Behe. All rights reserved. International copyright secured.

File Date: 9.24.96

This data file may be reproduced in its entirety for non-commercial use.

A return link to the Access Research Network web site (www.arn.org) would be appreciated.

www.ingramcontent.com/pod-product-compliance
Lightning Source LLC
Chambersburg PA
CBHW071623170426
43195CB00038B/2062